WITHDRAWN

The Alaska Boundary Dispute:
A Critical Reappraisal

THE FRONTENAC LIBRARY
GENERAL EDITOR—GEOFFREY MILBURN
Althouse College of Education
University of Western Ontario

Other titles in preparation

The Alaska Boundary Dispute:
A Critical Reappraisal

Norman Penlington

McGRAW-HILL RYERSON LIMITED
Toronto   Montreal   New York   London   Sydney
Mexico   Johannesburg   Panama   Düsseldorf
Singapore   Rio de Janeiro   New Delhi   Kuala Lumpur

THE ALASKA BOUNDARY DISPUTE: A CRITICAL REAPPRAISAL

Library of Congress Catalog Card Number 72-3862

ISBN 0-07-092957-2

1 2 3 4 5 6 7 8 9 10 AP-72 10 9 8 7 6 5 4 3 2

Printed and bound in Canada

ACKNOWLEDGMENTS

In a work of scholarship such as this, the author has had to make partial quotations from a large number of works public and private. Special thanks are due for the following:

Citations from *The John Charlton Papers,* University of Toronto Library, by permission of L. J. Curnoe.

Citations from A. E. Campbell, *Great Britain and the United States,* Longman, London, 1960, by permission of the publishers.

References to Carman Miller, *Minto and Canadian American Relations 1898-1904,* paper delivered at Canadian Historical Association Meetings, June, 1971, by permission of the author.

The Library of Congress, Washington, D.C., and the Public Archives of Canada, Ottawa, for their aid in the use of documents and atlases relating to the Alaska boundary dispute.

Maps by Mr. Sherman Hollander, Cartographer, Department of Geography, Michigan State University.

iv

Contents

Foreword

The books in the *Frontenac Library* present the findings of schol-
ars, not as established truths, but as well-considered opinions
designed to promote reflective search for understanding. While
discussing a particular topic or problem, each author refers to or
quotes from important original sources which are the raw ma-
terials of the historian's craft. At the same time, where other
interpretations exist, they are considered not necessarily as op-
posing theories but as significant contributions to the dimensions
of an issue. Wherever possible, the questions, methods, and procedures developed by sister disciplines in the humanities and
social sciences are used to adjust a focus too often predetermined
in the past by the constitutional viewpoint. In a very real sense,
we look over the shoulder of the historian to watch him handle
evidence and make judgments as he goes about that creative
task of writing which is the mark of his trade. Each volume in
the series is to be regarded as a responsible contribution to debate, an invitation to thought, and an opportunity for personal
assessment by the student.

The Alaska Boundary Dispute, the fifth volume in the *Frontenac Library,* satisfies all of these conditions. Although Dr.
Penlington's interest is focussed primarily on the period between
1896 and 1903, he has related events of those eight years to
developments of the previous century. His book is based upon a
thorough study of relevant sources in the three countries involved in an affair that influenced Canadian emotions, attitudes
and policies for many years.

Dr. Penlington has critically reviewed established opinions that
have become part of our national mythology. Before the signa-
tures on the final document were dry, Canadian politicians com-
can bullying and the anvil of British weakness. On this premise

vi

Canadian nationalists built an imposing structure that influenced not only relationships with the United States and Britain but also the intellectual development of three generations of our citizens. It is this interpretation that Dr. Penlington finds unacceptable. After a careful reassessment of contemporary evidence, he has put the Canadian record in a new perspective. From this reconstruction of interactions over a once remote section of the globe, we may gain insight about the national character at a dramatic formative period of our history.

G. Milburn

Preface

It is a platitude that a historian must be accurate and fair. It is less a platitude that one purpose of history is to hold up a mirror, as it were, not to Hamlet's "nature" but to the essential reality of a problem. To examine a problem on the surface is relatively easy, but to examine it in depth is difficult and often dangerous. It is difficult because to penetrate and explain the problems and the spirit of another age requires a fairness and a sympathy hard to come by. The historian must become aware not only of his own biases and assumptions but also of those of his own age and community. Only thus can he be relatively freed to face sympathetically the biases and assumptions of another age. It is dangerous because for the historian to soak himself in the spirit of another age is to expose himself to its emotional dangers. Yet failure to confront those dangers vitiates another purpose of history. "The truth shall make you free" is an ancient truism reconfirmed by modern depth psychology.

What has this truism to do with the bitter story of the Alaska boundary dispute and Canada? The truth shall make it free. Free from what? The frustration or hangup, as it is now popularly called, of a bitter experience. Free for what? Not to impose another pattern on itself but to let the country and its individuals creatively be. This does not mean repudiation of the country's past, like a youth widening the generation gap, for that would result in frustration in its opposite. It means rather that the energy imprisoned in past fears and shames is freed to strengthen its present.

How does this affect a country's relationships with its neighbours? A country with a deep frustration is an unfree country. Of course a country, like an individual, can never be completely free. Its experience, beliefs, and material setting, and its will to live, power, and wealth must all be considered when a leader guides his country, but always with his eye cocked on what other countries are doing. In ordinary circumstances it is difficult enough for a leader to guide his country, but it is extremely difficult when his country has suffered and repressed a frustration. The freer a country is from such a frustration, the more creative and constructive its leader's policy can be.

As always my debt is greatest to the staff of the Public Archives of Canada, especially to Mr. Peter Yurkiw, and for the loan of microfilms. I am indebted to the courteous assistance of the staff of Michigan State University Library, especially to Miss Eleanor Boyles, Documents Librarian; Mr. Francis X. Scannell, State Librarian of Michigan, for an extended loan; and Mr. H. B. Fant, Archivist, and Mr. Elmer O. Parker, Assistant Director, Old Military Records Division, National Archives, Washington. I am also grateful to Professor Alvin C. Gluek, Jr., of Erindale College, University of Toronto, for lending me microfilms of relevant Foreign Office papers; Mr. John A. Munro, Historian of the Department of External Affairs, for letting me have a copy of his *The Alaska Boundary Dispute* (1970) before publication; Mr. Sherman Hollander, Cartographer of the Department of Geography, Michigan State University, for the excellence of his maps; and my colleagues in the Department of Humanities, Professors DeWitt Platt and John Reinoehl, for suggestions of sources and interpretations for Chapter 1. My thanks for grants in aid are due to All University Research and to Professor Victor Hoar, Director, Canadian-American Studies Program. I am indebted also to Mary San Clemente for the final typing of the manuscript.

NORMAN PENLINGTON

East Lansing, January 1972

Chapter I

The Anglo-Russian Treaty of 1825: The Treaty Line and the Map Line

The decision of the Alaska Boundary Tribunal on October 20, 1903 set off one of the most concentrated explosions of resentment in twentieth-century Canadian history. Its magnitude, intensity, and effects call for explanation. Was Canada the victim of Lord Alverstone's weakness and contempt or victim of America's big stick? Is it strictly accurate to describe Canada as being sacrificed on the altar of Anglo-American friendship or was Canada essentially responsible for its own humiliation? These and other questions cannot be answered without an understanding of the origin and the nature of the Anglo-Russian Treaty of 1825, the disputes as to its interpretation, the decisions of the Tribunal of 1903, and the reasons for Canada's resentment for those decisions.

THE UKASE OF 1821

Until the eighteenth century the faraway northern Pacific region remained an area unknown to Europeans. Yet as early as the last decade of the fifteenth century it had been claimed by Spain as part of the western hemisphere under the Papal Bull of 1493 and the Treaty of Tordesillas with Portugal in 1494. Spain, however, made no attempt to enforce its claims until challenged in the eighteenth century. In that century European governments, moved by national interest and scientific curiosity, sent expeditions of exploration to that unexplored region of the world.

In 1741 Russia sent a Danish sea captain, Captain Vitus

1

Bering, who came upon the Aleutian Islands and sighted Mt. St. Elias on the continent of North America. He found those islands a valuable source of furs, for which there was a great demand in China. From the 1760s to the 1780s Britain sent Captain James Cook to solve the geographic puzzles of the Pacific area. In the 1790s Captain George Vancouver, who had been one of Cook's crew, meticulously surveyed and accurately mapped the Pacific coast line of northwest America. In 1793 Alexander Mackenzie, a trader and explorer for the North-West Fur Company, crossed overland from Great Slave Lake, thread-ed the Rocky Mountains, and reached the Pacific coast at about 52° N. lat. All three British explorers wrote extensive accounts of their explorations. Cook's account especially brought a host of fur traders to the northeast Pacific — particularly Yankee traders from New England after the American Revolution. In 1805 the United States also laid claim to the Pacific coast when President Jefferson secretly dispatched Meriwether Lewis and William Clark to the mouth of the Columbia River. Meanwhile Spain sought to revive its claims in the North Pacific, but gave up when it suffered diplomatic defeat from Britain at Nootka Sound. Britain had to withdraw its trading ships during the French Revolutionary and Napoleonic Wars, though its fur traders in the adjoining land area continued their activities. Thus until the outbreak of the War of 1812 Russians and Amer-icans contended for trade on the coast of northwest America.

The Russians, by means of fortified trading posts, controlled the areas of the best furs.[1] They themselves did not catch the animals but used the native Aleuts, whom they treated savagely and who responded in kind. Unfortunately the Russian Govern-ment on the other side of the world offered no protection to that native people. The government, however, did yield to the pressure of those traders whose business skill and court connec-tions sought to end destructive competition among Russian fur traders. Accordingly, by the Ukase (Edict) of 1799[2] the Emperor Paul granted the Russian-American Company a trading mono-poly across the Pacific Ocean from Asia to America, north of lat. 55°. South of lat. 55°, the company was empowered to ex-plore, settle, fortify, and trade with neighbouring peoples and exercise governmental powers. In return it was required to support the Orthodox Church and to encourage agriculture and shipbuilding. Although foreign governments were not informed of the Ukase, none of them — even after 1815 — protested against the scope or the exercise of the company's powers. Failure to do so was later interpreted by the Russian Government as tacit consent to the company's claims.

In spite of the considerable success of the Russian-American Company under its able and energetic manager — Alexander Baranoff (1799-1818) — its position was essentially weak. In northern latitudes provisions were scarce. In 1812, therefore, Baranoff sought a base for provisions and trade by establishing Fort Ross, in California, some eighty miles north of San Francisco Bay; and from 1815 to 1818 the Russians even tried to gain a foothold on the Hawaiian Islands; and for a few years too they were supplied with provisions by Americans from the Columbia River area.

American competition was a greater threat to the Russian company's success. Yankee traders on small vessels of 100 to 250 tons burden traded for a two-year period on the Pacific coast. In exchange for guns, whiskey, etc., — and harsh treatment of the frequently thieving and reluctant natives — these traders transported their profitable fur cargoes direct to Canton. Russian traders, however, were excluded from this direct trade "by some strange caprice of the Chinese",[3] being required to transport their furs overland from Siberia to China.

The Russian Government therefore protested to the American Government against the intrusion of Yankee traders. The American Government rejected the protest: the law of nations permitted trade in unsettled areas. In the meantime Russia, threatened by Napoleon, dropped the protest. After 1815 the economic prospects of the Russian company dwindled owing to the decline in the number of fur-bearing animals and excessive bureacratic interference from the Russian capital. The upshot of the company's protests against competition was the Emperor's Ukase of September 4/16, 1821. This Ukase extended the Russian-American Company's exclusive trading, whaling, and other economic privileges in the Pacific area to 51° in North America and 45°50' in Asia, and forbade foreign ships approaching the Asian or American coasts closer than 100 Italian miles. This provision came to be interpreted as making the Pacific Ocean a *mare clausum* (closed sea) to all but Russian shipping. Later on September 13/27, 1821, the Emperor Alexander renewed the company's charter and extended its territorial limits south from 55° to 51° N. lat.[4]

PROTESTS OF BRITAIN AND THE UNITED STATES AGAINST THE UKASE OF 1821

Superficially the protests of Britain and the United States against the Ukase of 1821 seem alike. The British Government protested against Russia's unprecedently extending its rights over waters 100 miles from the coast as contrary to the law of nations. It also denied Russian territorial claims on the American continent. The American Secretary of State, John Quincy Adams (1767-1848), made the same type of protest. Russia's maritime pretensions violated the doctrine of the freedom of the seas. As a New Englander, Adams would have known that the well-armed, well-manned, self-reliant Boston trader would not hesitate to fight for the right of unrestricted trade. Nor, he argued, had Russia any justification to claim territory as far south as 51° N. lat.

After some preliminary negotiations in London and Washington, the Russian Ambassadors were instructed to request that the representatives of the two countries at St. Petersburg be given full powers to negotiate a treaty in that city. Britain and the United States both complied. The British negotiator was Sir Charles Bagot (1781-1843), recently Minister to the United States and later Governor General of the Province of Canada (1841-43); and the United States appointed Henry Middleton (1770-1846), who had been Governor of South Carolina, Representative in Congress, and Minister to Russia (1820-30). Since British and American policy on both the maritime and territorial issues seemed the same, Secretary Adams suggested to Stratford Canning, the British Minister at Washington, the possibility of joint Anglo-American negotiations with Russia, modelled after the Anglo-American Convention of 1818. That Convention, which had a decisive influence in shaping the treaties of 1824 and 1825 and which has hitherto been insufficiently stressed, laid down that the boundary between the British and American territories west of the Lake of the Woods was the 49th parallel to the summit of the Rocky Mountains. In the area beyond the Rockies to the Pacific Ocean the claims of each power and "of any other Power or State" were to be recognized for ten years. This was not a joint, but an open, occupation treaty of the so-called Oregon territory. It conferred an advantage on the United States because four months later — in February, 1819 — the United States secured Spanish claims on the Pacific coast north of 42° N. lat. in the transcontinental treaty with Spain. So far as Adams was concerned the object of both the treaties of 1818 and 1819 was to push the recognized boundaries of the United States through to the Pacific Ocean.[5]

George Canning, the new British Foreign Secretary, was also a nationalist and economic imperialist who envisaged a great transpacific trade between the Oregon and the Orient. But in the 1820s his policy lacked strong national support because English opinion and English policy were beginning to move in a free-trade and anti-imperialist direction. Nevertheless he was an ardent supporter of Hudson's Bay Company interests on the Pacific coast, consulted its officials, and followed many of its suggestions in the ensuing Anglo-Russian negotiations. Thus Stratford Canning recommended to his cousin, the Foreign Secertary, George Canning, the acceptance of Secretary Adam's proposals. George Canning liked the possibility of maritime co-operation but was wary of territorial co-operation. Though Adams asserted that the United States claim did not extend beyond 51° N. lat., which was two degrees north of the 49th parallel that American commissioners had offered in 1818, a tripartite territorial agreement would hardly work to Britain's advantage. Adams' strategy was to play off Britain and Russia against one another in northwest America. Russia, too, could exploit Anglo-American differences.

But the settlement of northwestern American problems to all three powers in 1823 was secondary to the recognition of the independence of the Latin American republics and the possibility of their suppression by the reactionary powers of Europe assisting in the restoration of Spanish power in Latin America. The overthrow by a French army of the liberal government of Spain raised this possibility. Accordingly in the summer of 1823 when Richard Rush (1780-1859), the American Minister to Britain, was discussing outstanding Anglo-American issues, he asked Canning whether Britain would let the emancipation of the Spanish colonies continue. At the next interview Canning replied with a proposal for a joint Anglo-American declaration on the Spanish colonies which would leave the question of recognition open and oppose any transfer of territory. Rush agreed provided Britain recognize the independence of the Latin-American republics first. Canning refused on grounds that recognition was premature. Britain was interested in enlisting United States help in maintaining the European balance of power. Adams had no interest in that policy any more than Canning had in support of United States policy of recognition in Latin America.

This divergence of interest widened when Canning learned details of American policy. After Canning inquired of Rush on United States policy in northwest America before he sent instructions to Sir Charles Bagot, he learned that the United States claim reached not 51° but "north of 55°." Accordingly Canning at once wrote to Rush. "Do the United States mean to travel north between us and Russia?" [That is, cut Britain off from the Pacific.] Rush replied "it was even so." American policy was more fully disclosed a few days later when news of what later came to be called the Monroe Doctrine arrived. The words, "the American continents . . . are henceforth not to be considered as subjects for future colonization by any European power," angered the nationalistic Canning. This Non-Colonization Principle for Canning was a diplomatic defeat, because it suggested that the United States rather than Britain was defending Latin America from reactionary aggression. In fact on October 9, 1823, Canning had obtained the pledge of the French Ambassador to London not to obtain territory or use force in Latin America. The Non-Colonization Principle, however, gave Canning an excuse for separate rather than joint negotiations with Russia.[6] Canning suspected Adams of trying to gratify Russia at Britain's expense on land and Britain at Russia's expense at sea, a suspicion which was largely true. Thus in his instructions of January 24, 1824, to Bagot, after reciting American actions inimical to Britain, Canning was mainly concerned with

explaining Britain's refusal to act jointly with the United States
in negotiations with Russia. When published the instructions
would of course justify Canning's policy. Canning also instructed Bagot to conclude negotiations with Russia before the United
States did so.[7]

THE RUSSIAN-AMERICAN TREATY OF 1824
AND THE ANGLO-RUSSIAN TREATY OF 1825

In the previous summer (1823) there had been preliminary
Anglo-Russian negotiations. Bagot had asserted that the British
claim extended to 59° N. lat., but he conceded that 57° N. lat.
would be satisfactory. The line would thus go along Cross
Sound, up Lynn Canal, and continue on the 135th meridian to
the Arctic Ocean. The Russian negotiators, Count Nesselrode,
the Russian Foreign Minister, and Pierre de Poletica, former
Russian Minister to the United States, claimed that the Russian
boundary followed an unspecified meridian to the Arctic Ocean,
but excluded the mouth of the Mackenzie River, which was the
best fur-trapping area in North America. Throughout the negotiations, however, the Russians insisted that the line begin at
55° N. lat.

Why were the British never able to budge the Russians from
the starting point of 55° N. lat.? The Emperor Alexander was
determined to maintain the prestige of his father — the Emperor Paul — who in the Ukase of 1799 had granted the Russian-American Company trading rights as far south as 55° N.
lat. Professor Stuart R. Tompkins treats this as a "face-saving
issue." But this was the kind of issue to which Alexander would
cling, for after 1815 he became reactionary. In the Russian-
American treaty of 1824 his apparent influence is shown by his
insistence on the exclusion of trade with the natives in liquor
as well as in firearms. Most important Count Nesselrode discerned the weak point of the British claim: the Anglo-American
agreement of 1818 waiving sovereignty west of the Rockies for
ten years. Since Adams had instructed Middleton on July 22,
1823, to agree to the Russian claim of 55° N. lat., it is not impossible that Russia also learned of it or guessed its existence.

Serious Anglo-Russian negotiations began in February, 1824.

Bagot opened the negotiations by offering a line beginning at 56° N. lat. on Chatham Strait going north to Lynn Canal, turning northwest to Mt. St. Elias and thence on the 140th meridian to the Arctic. Russia countered with her usual line at 55°, which was now adjusted to 54°40' to include all of Prince of Wales Island, across the sea, up Portland Canal, north to the mountains it was assumed paralleled the "sinuosities of the coast" — the first appearance of this famous phrase — to the 139th meridian, and thence north to the Arctic. All subsequent British offers and Russian counter offers came to a meridian of longitude along which the boundary went to the Arctic Ocean. British subjects were also to be allowed perpetual navigation and trade on the strip and trade with Sitka (Novo-Archangelsk). But each time Bagot conceded a more southerly starting line he strove to confine Russian territory closer to the coast and to keep the meridian as far west from the mouth of the Mackenzie River as possible. Bagot's next concession began at 55½°, went slightly north, turned east on Sumner Strait to the coast and to a ten-league line — the first reference to this distance — and thence northwest to the 140th meridian. To this the Russians made no concession. Bagot now offered his fourth and "ultimate proposition," starting again farther south at 54°40'. But instead of going east to Portland Canal, it turned north on Clarence Strait, and thence east on Sumner Strait to the ten-degree line, and so on as in the previous line. It was this fourth concession of Bagot that Judge Gray, the Executive Council of British Columbia, and the British Commissioners of 1898 at the Joint High Commission advanced as the boundary claim of Canada. Nor did the Russians make any concessions to this offer. Unauthorized to exceed his boundary instructions, Bagot now sought to settle the maritime question by itself. But Nesselrode refused to settle that question prior to the boundary question. On March 17/29, 1824, Bagot therefore angrily referred the question back to London.[8]

At the same time as the Anglo-Russian negotiations were coming to a standstill, Russian-American negotiations were proceeding successfully. The Russians ignored the Non-Colonization Principle of the Monroe Doctrine and proposed settlement on a basis of mutual interest. Middleton offered to recognize

55° N. lat. as Russia's southern boundary, in return for Russia's giving up the maritime exclusion and granting Americans trading privileges on the coast. Russia accepted this bargain. On April 5/17, 1824, the Russian-American Convention was signed. Under it individuals of both powers could fish, trade, and land on any shore of the Pacific Ocean, except in occupied parts, which could only be resorted to by permission of the occupying powers. On the Pacific coast of North America, latitude 54°40' was to divide the Russian and American zones, or spheres of influence, as they would have been termed later. Finally, individuals of both powers, though prohibited from forming establishments in the zones of the other, could fish and trade, except in "firearms and firewater" in the zones of the other for ten years.[9]

In the summer of 1824 Anglo-Russian negotiations moved a step forward when George Canning conceded the Russian demand of 54°40' with the line crossing east to Portland Canal up to the 56th latitude and along the seaward base of the mountains following the sinuosities of the coast, and thence to the 139th degree of longitude. Count Lieven, the Russian Ambassador in London, protested that the word "base" was vague and might mean the water's edge, and preferred as the boundary the "summit" of a "chain of mountains." Canning agreed. But when Bagot submitted the Canning-Lieven agreement for signature and ratification, Nesselrode demanded the reduction of trading rights at Sitka and on the strip from perpetuity to ten years. Perpetuity, he argued, was contrary to sovereignty. Bagot suspended negotiations again for the same reasons as earlier: the concessions demanded exceeding his instructions.[10] Bagot's long-time request to be transferred as Ambassador from St. Petersburg was now acceded to.

The British policy of conciliation with Russia having failed, Canning now decided to use against Russia its own horse-trading tactics, of which Bagot had so bitterly complained. This opinion concerning the aggressiveness of British tactics appears to contradict George Canning's oft-quoted instructions of December 8, 1824, to his cousin Stratford Canning, who took Bagot's place as plenipotentiary. The settlement of territorial limits, George Canning instructed Stratford Canning, was

proposed by us only as a mode . . . [to enable] the court of

Russia, under cover of the more comprehensive arrangement, to withdraw, with less appearance of concession, the offensive pretensions of that edict.

This and similar indications were used by the United States in its argument before the Alaska Boundary Tribunal of 1903 to prove that Britain's prime interest in the Anglo-Russian Treaty of 1825 was maritime and not territorial.

There are four objections to this contention. In the first place documentary evidence of the negotiations for the treaty shows far more concern with territorial than maritime issues. Obviously the larger the British territory the more it would facilitate the trading operations of the Hudson's Bay Company. In the second place statements of the foreign secretary were justifications for his future published record as the Russian Ambassador acutely noted about Canning's documents.[11] In the third place the aggressive tactics in forcing Russia to agree to a treaty worked. In the fourth place Russia was very angry at their use and strove — successfully — to undo one of its objectionable concessions to Britain.

Negotiations now moved to success. Stratford Canning was instructed to concede the ten-year limitation on trade with Sitka and on the strip, for Britain now knew that the United States had only ten-year trading rights. Apparently as an outgrowth of Bagot's suggestion that, since Russia was to receive all of Prince of Wales Island, Britain should receive a longitudinal concession — a concession Count Lieven had agreed to — Stratford Canning was instructed to demand not 139° but 141° W. long. Canada received the Klondike as a result of that concession. In spite of Count Lieven's agreements in London, the Russian negotiators in St. Petersburg objected to the ten-league limitation on the width of the strip preferring a width bounded by the crest of the mountains only. The frequency of Russian objections almost suggests a desire not to sign a treaty at all. But Britain's insistence on the ten-league limitation, the demand for 141° W. long., and the threat to make difficulties, if Russia would not sign, evidently forced Russia to agree to the Anglo-Russian Convention of February 16/28, 1825.

THE TREATY LINE AND THE MAP LINE

From the British public's point of view Article I was the key article. It laid down the right of British and Russian citizens to navigate, trade, and fish in the northern Pacific area under certain conditions. Thus without directly saying so, Russia abrogated the maritime provision of the Ukase of 1821. This and the second article against illicit navigating and fishing were essentially the same as the first two articles in the Russian-American Convention. From the point of view of the future boundary controversy, Articles III and IV were the key articles. Since much of the argument at the Alaska Boundary Tribunal of 1903 turned on the meaning of phrases in those two articles, they must be quoted in full:

> III. The line of demarcation between the Possessions of the High Contracting Parties, upon the Coast of the Continent, and the Islands of America to the North-West, shall be drawn in the manner following:
>
> Commencing from the Southernmost Point of the Island called *Prince of Wales* Island, which Point lies in the parallel of 54 degrees 40 minutes North latitude, and between 131st and 133rd degrees of West longitude (Meridian of Greenwich), the said line shall ascend to the North along the channel called *Portland Channel,* as far as the Point of the Continent where it strikes the 56th degree of North latitude; from this last-mentioned Point, the line of demarcation shall follow the summit of the mountains situated parallel to the coast, as far as the point of intersection of the 141st degree of West longitude (of the same Meridian); and, finally, from the said point of intersection, the said Meridian Line of the 141st degree, in its prolongation as far as the Frozen Ocean, shall form the limit between Russian and British Possessions on the Continent of America to the North-West.
>
> IV. With reference to the line of demarcation laid down in the preceding Article, it is understood:
>
> 1st. That the Island called *Prince of Wales* Island shall belong wholly to Russia.

2nd. That wherever the summit of the mountains which extend in a direction parallel to the Coast, from the 56th degree of North latitude to the point of intersection of the 141st degree of West longitude, shall prove to be at the distance of more than ten marine leagues from the Ocean, the limit between the British Possessions and the line of Coast which is to belong to Russia, as above mentioned, shall be formed by a line parallel to the windings of the Coast, and which shall never exceed the distance of ten marine leagues therefrom.[12]

Russia, however, continued to be angry at the ten-league limitation on the width of the lisière (a French word meaning selvage — the edge of cloth). At the time of the exchange of treaty ratifications in April, 1825, Count Lieven complained to George Canning

how ungracious the refusal of the English Government to consent to the establishment of the frontier by means of the crest of the mountains which follow the sinuosities of the coast, must appear to the Imperial Cabinet when it was merely a question of the occupation of a few leagues of land more or less, and when an immense extent of desert country still separates us from the English possessions.

Russia's anger evidently had some bearing on the Russian Admiralty's decision in 1826 to publish with names in the Russian language a map of northwestern America showing a boundary line ten-leagues distant from the coast though the 141st meridian was drawn according to the treaty. In the following year (1827), the Russian Government issued essentially the same map with the same boundary but this time with names in French — the language of diplomatists. This map was given official sanction by the notation "publié par ordre de sa Majesté Imperiale." (Map on p. 13.) While it is conceivable that Britain missed seeing the Russian Admiralty map of 1826, it is inconceivable that it missed the map of 1827. Britain did not protest this "map" line (as this book shall call it). This map line was the boundary line that the United States understood

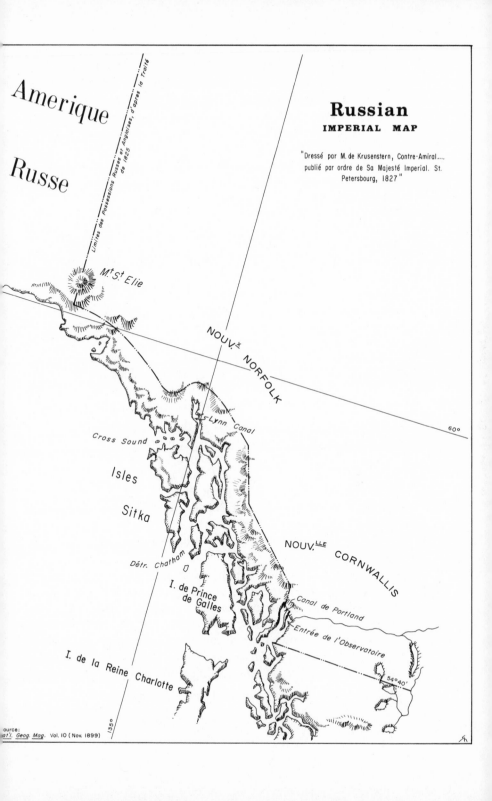

Amerique

Russe

Limites des Possessions Russes et Anglaises, d'après la Traité de 1825

Mt. St. Elie

NOUV.x NORFOLK

60°

Lynn Canal

Cross Sound

Isles

Sitka

NOUV.lle CORNWALLIS

Détr. Chatham

I. de Prince
de Galles

Canal de Portland

Entrée de l'Observatoire

I. de la Reine Charlotte

54°40'

135°

Russian
IMPERIAL MAP

"Dressé par M. de Krusenstern, Contre-Amiral....
publié par ordre de Sa Majesté Imperial. St.
Petersbourg, 1827 "

ource:
a'l. Geog. Mag. Vol. 10 (Nov. 1899)

when it purchased Alaska in 1867. Indeed, it was essentially the boundary line of the decisions of 1903 and 1905.[13]

Why did Britain not protest the map line, which was contrary to the "treaty" line (as this book shall call it), that is the line designated in the treaty? If Britain had complained that the Russian map line violated the treaty line, the Russians might very well have retorted, where would you draw the line? This would have necessitated, as a preliminary to settlement, an expensive, joint, and probably inadequate survey, in view of primitive surveying techniques, which the British Parliament would hardly have financed. In any case Russia's assertion of the ten-league line, if unprotested, would mollify Russia's anger. In making a ten-league limitation on the Pacific coast boundary in his instructions to Stratford Canning, George Canning stated his hope to avoid the boundary difficulties of the mountains on the Atlantic coast, which were found to be situated differently on the maps. In the negotiations for the treaty of 1825 the insistence of a boundary line on the crest of mountains nearest the sea seemed to have partly served the purpose of forcing Russia to come to an agreement. Furthermore Bagot had first proposed the ten-league line. Under these conditions does not the failure of Britain to protest against the Russian assertion of the ten-league line even suggest that Britain envisaged that possibility?

Once Britain had acquiesced in the Russian interpretation of the treaty of 1825, sixty years of map precedents unanimously fortified the interpretation. Of those maps there need only be mentioned four, two drawn in Canada. As early as 1831 Joseph Bouchette, the deputy surveyor-general of Lower Canada, published in London a map of North America which closely followed the boundary of the Russian map. In 1857 a map drawn by order of Joseph Cauchon, Canadian Commissioner of Crown Lands, did likewise.[14]

An unprotested line on maps might be considered an implicit acknowledgment of the Russian interpretation. But a few official and explicit British actions and statements confirmed that interpretation. After the signing of the Treaty of 1825 the Hudson's Bay Company showed great energy in exploiting the terms of the treaty. The Russians, alarmed at its success, decided to thwart its activities by establishing a Russian post at the mouth of the Stikine River. In 1834 the Russians stopped a Hudson's Bay ship — the *Dryad* — carrying supplies to build a post farther up the river. In the long diplomatic wrangle that ensued between British and Russian authorities over the incident, the Hudson's Bay Company first demanded damages, which Russia refused to pay. Eventually the matter was smoothed over by the Russian-American Company secretly leasing the strip to the Hudson's Bay Company for ten years. It promised to pay the Russian Company 2,000 land-otter skins per year, sell 5,000 per year at a fixed rate to the Russians at Sitka, supply the Russians with provisions and better grade English manufactured goods, and forgo all claims connected with the *Dryad* incident.[15]

During the Crimean War, 1854-55, the British and Russian authorities neutralized their North American possessions. In 1857 a British Parliamentary Committee investigated the Hudson's Bay Company monopoly and Sir George Simpson, its governor, in discussing the neutrality agreement observed:

> The British territory runs along inland from the coast about 30 miles; the Russian territory runs along the coast; we have the rights of navigation through the rivers to hunt the interior country.[16]

The Parliamentary Committee also published two maps showing possession by Russia of a continuous strip of land shutting off British territory from the sea.

Apart from the ten-league Russian interpretation, what are we to think of the treaty itself? John S. Galbraith, the author of *The Hudson's Bay Company as an Imperial Factor* (1957), thought it a successful treaty. Stuart R. Tompkins in his article "Drawing the Alaskan Boundary" (1945) thought Britain did badly because of failure to budge Russia from latitude 54°40'. But Tompkins was unrealistic to expect expansionist Russia and the United States in the 1820s to accept contemporary British diplomatic standards of conciliation — the standards of the then most powerful nation. Undoubtedly the Anglo-American Convention of 1818 and the Russian-American Convention of 1824 were intended as limitations on Britain's power in the Pacific area. Tompkins recognized but insufficiently stressed the influence of these conventions. Given these limitations, this writer thinks that Britain did very well in the Anglo-Russian Convention of 1825. The maritime provision was abrogated and Britain gained a good boundary — particularly regarding the ten-league limitation — which probably protected Canada from a much less favourable boundary line in 1903.

Implicit in Tompkins' analysis seems to be the lament of a Canadian still smarting over the decision of 1903: if only British territory could have reached the sea. But in the treaty of 1825 there is no ground for such a Canadian might-have-been. Even if the summits of presumed mountains parallel to the coast designated in the treaty of 1825 could have been found in the 1820s, the line would have not crossed the heads of inlets but encircled them. For in 1825 both the British and the Russian negotiators intended, and in 1867 the United States understood, that the lisière, regardless of its width, formed an unbroken point of support for Russia's island archipelago and cut British territory off from the sea.

Canada's Diplomatic Challenge
to the Map Line 1872-1895

So long as the Alaska boundary area remained the haunt of Indians and fur traders under the authority of the Hudson's Bay Company, boundaries meant little. But once the sovereignty of states replaced the sway of fur companies, and economic, social and religious developments gave sinew to sovereignty, the need for a fixed boundary kept growing. The United States purchase of Alaska from Russia in 1867 marked the beginning of this process, if not its elimination; for purchase was also intended to strengthen United States influence in British Columbia with a view to its annexation.

THE UNITED STATES AND THE TERRITORY
OF ALASKA 1867-1897

The Russian-American Convention of 1867 described the eastern boundary of Alaska "as established by the convention between Russia and Great Britain in February 28-16, 1825."[1] The Secretary of State, William E. Seward, ordered the publication of a map (see p. 18), the eastern boundaries of which closely followed the Russian map line, which continued to be copied by the cartographers of the world for most of the next two decades. Nor did Britain protest the exercise of United States sovereignty within the strip, though the visit of a United States naval vessel to the island archipelago was little more than token sovereignty. This tepid visit reflects the considerable American indifference if not scorn for the purchase of "Seward's Ice Box," as hostile critics put it.

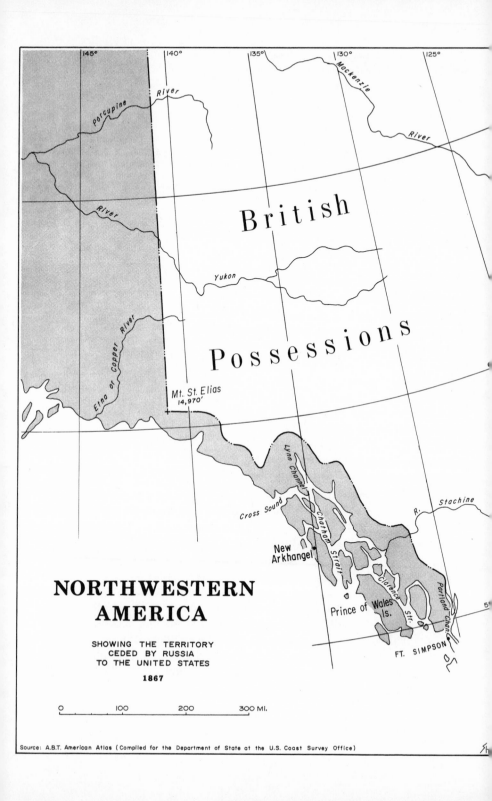

145° 140° 135° 130° 125°

Porcupine River

Mackenzie River

River

British

Yukon

River

Elno of Copper River

Mt. St. Elias
14,970'

Possessions

Lynn Channel

Cross Sound

Chatham Strait

R. Stachine

New Arkhangel

Clarence Str.

Portland Channel

NORTHWESTERN
AMERICA

Prince of Wales Is.

SHOWING THE TERRITORY
CEDED BY RUSSIA
TO THE UNITED STATES

1867

FT. SIMPSON

O   100   200   300 MI.

Source: A.B.T. American Atlas (Compiled for the Department of State at the U.S. Coast Survey Office)

Alaska was certainly forbidding in those days. The Panhandle, which is the principal concern of this book, juts down 500 miles from Alaska proper and averages 35 miles in width from the coast on the edge of the continent. In area, it extends 25,000 square miles, 14,000 of which comprise the islands, varying in size from a few square yards to about 6,000 square miles. Rugged mountains cover the Panhandle; and on the continental strip they rise 6,000 to 15,000 feet in height. They also drop abruptly into the sea and form fiords, the most famous of which in the 1890s was Lynn Canal which provided the easiest access to passes leading to the Yukon. These formidable mountain barriers are also broken on the east by two main rivers — the Taku and the Stikine — but they also protect the coastal area from Arctic winds. On the other hand the prevailing westerlies and the "Black Current", flowing across the Pacific from Japan, moderate temperatures and bring heavy rain and fog. The Panhandle is thus well-forested with a thick undergrowth, and hence an area where fur-bearing animals abounded; and fish — especially salmon — are plentiful in rivers and fiords. The mountains also contain extensive ore bodies — gold, copper, quartz, and gypsum. But these resources, the rugged terrain, the narrow living space — Juneau extends over the water — permit only a small population in the Panhandle.[2]

On its purchase Alaska did not become a typical American territory normally preparing for statehood, but remained an anomalous political district placed under the shadowy authority of the War Department. Some 500 soldiers stationed in six Alaskan posts served under military law, while the rest of the population dwelt in anarchy. The result was disorder and crime recalling the Russian experience of 100 years earlier. The Indians were debauched by bad liquor, and committed assaults on the white population. The force of soldiers had to leave the malefactors unpunished; it lacked ships to catch them; and finally in 1877 it was withdrawn. Thus the problem was not misgovernment, but absence of government. By 1879 the whites, terrified at being outnumbered by the Indians, petitioned Washington for protection in vain. Desperate, they appealed to Victoria. British naval authorities dispatched a sloop to Sitka where it remained until a United States ship provided relief. As a result of this incident Alaska was placed under the Treasury and Navy Departments, a change that brought greater stability.

These economic and social developments showed that Alaska now needed the institutions of the modern state. Initially the economic interests of Alaska had centred and long continued in the fur trade. Meanwhile the decline of the whaling industry in the 1870s accounted for the transfer of capital to the salmon fishing industry. By 1880 big companies controlled the industry, although the first canning factory had only been established on Prince of Wales Island two years earlier. Gold mining had flourished in the 1870s, and by the early 1880s the Treadwell Mining Company had been established at Juneau. This economic activity increased the population, and consequently the demand for civil government. Taking the lead were religious denominations, which in the 1870s had founded mission stations and schools. The lobbying of missionaries in Congress succeeded in overcoming the opposition of business interests, which feared increased population, taxation, and regulation. Accordingly in 1884 Congress passed an "Organic Act," which provided civil government for Alaska. But in fact it was the sketchiest of government and proved inadequate for the large and often lawless population that poured into and across the Panhandle in 1898 during the Yukon Gold Rush. This inrush of population also testified to the necessity of a boundary settlement.

BRITISH COLUMBIA AND A BOUNDARY SETTLEMENT

Within five years of the purchase of Alaska, pressure for a boundary settlement came from the adjoining Province of British Columbia on account of a gold strike in its northern Cassiar district. On receiving this request of the British Columbia Legislature for a settlement, through the normal diplomatic channels — the Dominion Government, Governor General, Colonial Office, Foreign Office, and the British Minister in Washington — Sir Edward Thornton raised the question with the Secretary of State, Hamilton Fish. This roundabout, time-consuming channel was the result of Canada's still being a colony with the machinery and, to some extent, the substance of its external affairs controlled by Britain. In December, 1872, President U. S. Grant recommended, in his annual message to Congress, the appointment of a commission acting jointly with a British commission to determine the Alaska boundary while a sparse population lessened the possibility of border conflict. Congress did nothing; a survey was too costly. Whereupon Britain proposed marking points on rivers, but even this proposal was rejected for the same reason.[3]

Traffic on the Stikine River — the only practicable route to the Cassiar Mountains — made a boundary settlement urgent. The Treaty of Washington of 1871 had restricted the free movement of British subjects permitted under the Anglo-Russian Treaty of 1825 to movement for commercial purposes only. In 1873 the customs official stationed at the mouth of the Stikine even prohibited the exercise of that right on the ground that the American Government forbade it. Canada retaliated by forbidding American vessels carrying goods between Canadian ports unless they first called at an American port. Next year Washington relaxed the prohibition on the Stikine.

On the other hand in 1875 local American and Canadian customs collectors came to an accommodation. Without reporting the matter to their superiors they fixed a line on the Stikine River a short distance below the trading post of a successful British trader. The superior of the American collector on learning of this arrangement protested: it violated presumed American territory. The trading post was thereupon moved up river. In the following year a more serious difficulty occurred. A convicted criminal, a naturalized American citizen named Peter Martin, in his transfer from Cassiar to Victoria, attempted to escape and severely assaulted one of his guards. He was convicted of this assault in Victoria. But United States authorities protested the conviction and demanded Martin's release: the transfer and the assault had taken place on American territory.[4]

Two weeks before this protest, Justice J. H. Gray, a New Brunswick Father of Confederation and a Macdonald appointee to the British Columbia Supreme Court, had written to the premier, Alexander Mackenzie, complaining of the legal and economic difficulties caused by an unmarked boundary. Gray's own experience in the area [he had held assizes at Cassiar] made him certain that a coastal range rose within fifteen miles of the sea. This range would constitute the boundary under the Treaty of 1825: it would also reduce the width of the strip and enlarge British mineral claims.[5] This belated re-assertion of the treaty line had considerable influence on Canadian and British leaders.

Meanwhile the confusion of an unmarked frontier and the United States reluctance to fix the boundary moved Canadian authorities to make an attempt. One of its surveyors, Joseph Hunter, was instructed to fix a provisional boundary on the Stikine River. He did so, and also reported finding the mountain range described in the treaty of 1825 about nineteen miles in a direct line from the coast. He also advised the government that Peter Martin's assault had occurred within American territory: whereupon Martin was released. In 1878, on the suggestion of the British Minister, Hunter's line was accepted by the Secretary of State, William M. Evarts, without prejudice to any future settlement.[6] Thus for the first time the United States had officially acknowledged that there might be an alternative to the ten-league map line.

The decline of the Cassiar goldfields temporarily diminished pressure for a boundary settlement.

CHALLENGE TO THE MAP LINE

With the exception of Justice Gray's and the Canadian Government's claims, and Hunter's line on the Stikine River, it had hitherto been assumed in Canada that the ten-league map line was the treaty line. In 1874, for example, the British Columbia Legislature referred to the boundary as some thirty miles from the coast.[7] J. S. Dennis, the Surveyor-General of Canada, drew a ten-league boundary line for a map published in the *Canada Sessional Papers* of 1878. But in 1884 British Columbia pressure for a boundary settlement began again, not for the map line but for the presumed treaty line. Justice Gray's ideas on the Portland Channel were now being accepted by the British Columbia Executive Council. Gray claimed that the true line started at Cape Chacon, ran north on Clarence Strait up Behm Canal, where it struck the 56th parallel, proceeded to the summits, and turning northwest followed "at or within ten marine leagues from the coast" until it intersected the 141st meridian. This claim marked on a British Columbia map of 1884 was based on the theory that in later editions of the Anglo-Russian Treaty of 1825 the words "Portland Canal" had crept into Article IV following the phrase "the said line shall ascend to the north along the passage called Portland Canal." By omitting "Portland Canal" Gray's suggestion seemed plausible. Unfortunately the phrase "Portland Canal" did appear in the original treaty. But this inconvenient fact did not prevent the Canadian Government in 1898 from inadvisedly adopting Gray's untenable theory. Indeed between 1884 and 1903 maps published by British Columbia and Canada called attention to the growth of their claims in Alaska.[8]

In the same year [1884] Dr. W. H. Dall of the United States Coast and Geodetic Survey wrote to Dr. George M. Dawson, the Director of the Geological Survey of Canada: the Alaska boundary question should be "stirred up" before trouble arose. Since the area lacked a natural boundary the United States would have to rely on the ten-league line paralleling the windings of the coast. This would be impossible to trace over a " 'sea of mountains' ": it would cross itself in many places, as he later wrote. Therefore a committee of Canadian-American geographers should be set up to survey the disputed area and draft a new treaty laying down "determinable boundaries."[9] Though Canadian and Colonial Office officials saw the letter, Dr. Dall received no reply.

In December, 1885, in his first annual message to Congress, President Grover Cleveland using many of the same arguments recommended a preliminary survey, though Congress as usual did nothing. The President also announced that he had invited Britain to consider a "more convenient line." After some discussion with the British Foreign Secretary, Lord Salisbury, the American Minister, Edward J. Phelps, informed him of the American proposal: a joint commission to determine the boundary. Though personally favourable Salisbury would take no action without consulting Canada.

The Canadian Governor General and the Prime Minister were skeptical and suspicious of this proposal. Lord Lansdowne

observed that, because of the United States record in its deal-
ings with Canada, the duties of the commission be narrowed
to making a survey only, otherwise it would haggle "over every
inch of ground." Sir John Macdonald agreed. Macdonald
wrote to Sir Charles Tupper, the High Commissioner in London,
that Canada should wait until Congress voted the money and
that the proposed American line would surrender valuable
territory containing minerals. To Lord Lansdowne he explained
Canada's wish "to secure an ocean port for Canada along that
coast." Having "suffered so much in all negotiations with the
United States," British America should "take care not to be
cheated again."[10]

With the approval of Lord Lansdowne and two former Gov-
ernors General, the Canadian Government recommended to the
Colonial Office for the study of the problem, Colonel D. R.
Cameron, who had been associated with Canadian boundary
questions since the early 1870s. In a series of reports to the
Colonial Office on the boundary question Cameron's contentions
had a big influence on future British claims. He contended that
the "correct location" of the boundary line on the strip was
"over the tops of the mountains nearest the sea." These mountains did not refer to a continuous range — a word that does
not appear in the treaty — nor to a watershed, for the rivers
rose in the interior and crossed the strip. Nor did it matter,
Cameron argued, if the line, following the crests of the "first
mountain range," was broken by inlets and fiords provided their
mouths were less than six miles wide: for such inlets according
to international law were "territorial" and "cease to be part of
the ocean."[11] He also argued that in the treaty the word "coast"
referred not to the coast of the inlets, but to that of the ocean.
Cameron therefore concluded that the line crossed the inlets
and did not go round their heads as the United States claimed.
Cameron dismissed Justice Gray's thesis that the Portland Canal
line ran up Clarence Strait and the United States assertion that
it ran along what Vancouver had renamed Observatory Inlet.
Portland Channel, the renamed Observatory Inlet, first appeared on an Admiralty map of 1853 made by an unknown
authority[12] and copied by later map makers. Vancouver, on the
contrary, had originally designated as Portland Canal the chan-

nel north of the four islands in Portland Inlet, as the body of water on both sides of the islands came to be known.

Cameron therefore concluded that Britain should disavow what this book calls the "map line", because the treaty made the location of the dividing line "dependent on alternative circumstances, the occurrence or the non-occurrence of mountains." While Cameron admitted that the United States might take the map line as a tacit admission of the correctness of the United States claim, the United States itself had not hesitated to deny boundary arguments founded on tacit consent.[13]

Cameron's thesis was a formidable and subtle piece of treaty interpretation, worthy of a Philadelphia lawyer. It was based on a legalistic interpretation of the treaty line — the line described in the treaty. To distinguish it from the treaty line and the map line we might call it an "interpreted" line, which was advocated in various forms by Canadians in most negotiations. The important point to note about this line as distinguished from the presumed treaty line was that it allowed Canada access to the sea. But this interpreted line had no warrant in the intention of the treaty makers nor support from precedent.

But as Canadians learned of this and similar interpretations their appetite for Alaskan territory continued to grow, as the maps on pages 26-29 record. It was not simply a coincidence that British Guiana claims to territory disputed with Venezuela, as recorded in the maps of Colonial Office Year Books in the 1880s, also grew.[14] Both appetites partly reflect the spirit of imperialist expansion of the late nineteenth century. The State Department would have known of both sets of maps. Did it see a pattern of British expansion? Did the claim in Alaska contribute to the Venezuela Incident?

THE CANADIAN GOVERNMENT AND A BOUNDARY SETTLEMENT

The foregoing interest in the whereabouts of a boundary was not shared by the Joint High Commission of 1887-1888, which had been summoned primarily to settle the Atlantic fisheries question. Though the Alaska boundary question was relegated to unimportance it was considered. Joseph Chamberlain, the

BRITISH COLUMBIAN AND

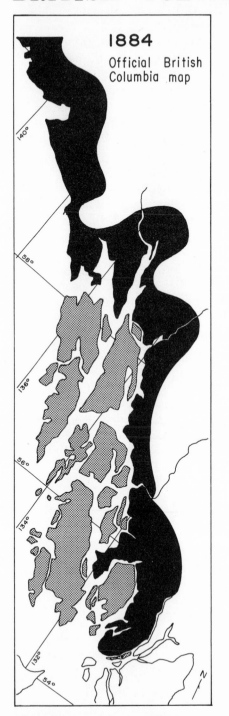

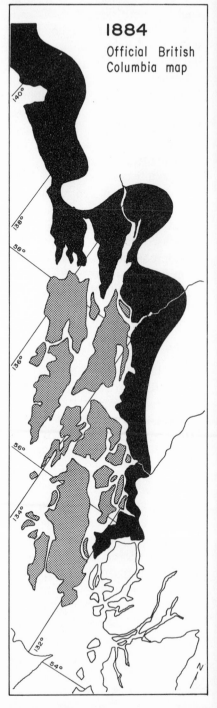

□ British   ▨ American on the Archipelago

CANADIAN CLAIMS, 1884-1903

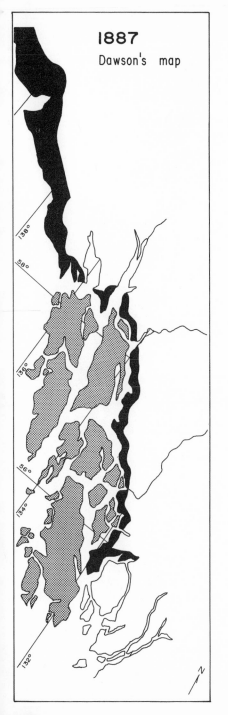

1887
Dawson's map

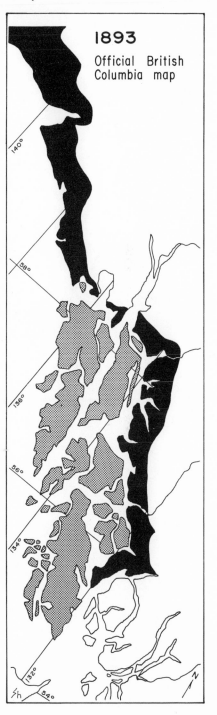

1893
Official British Columbia map

American on the Continent

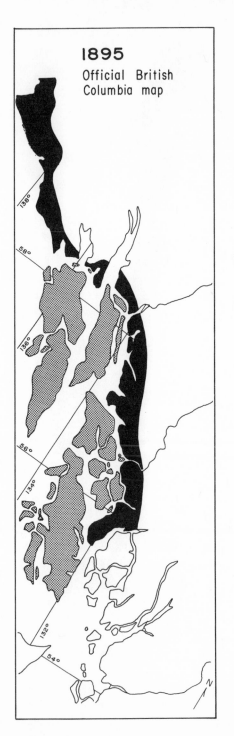

1895
Official British
Columbia map

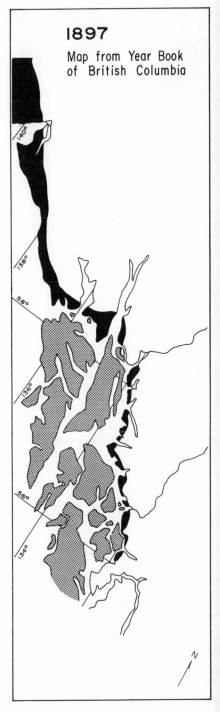

1897
Map from Year Book
of British Columbia

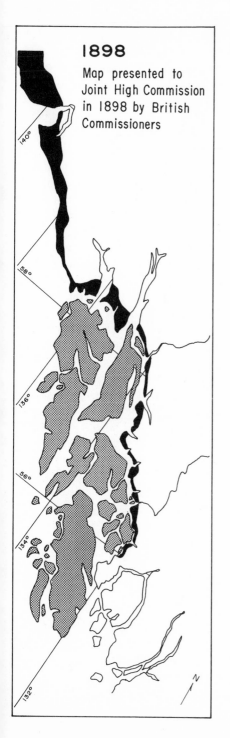

1898

Map presented to
Joint High Commission
in 1898 by British
Commissioners

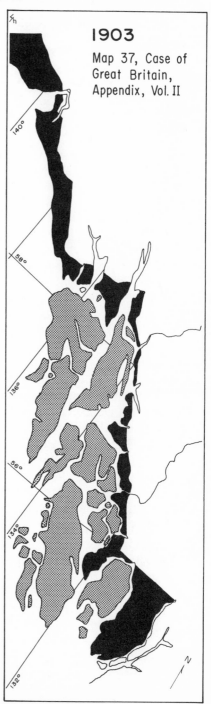

1903

Map 37, Case of
Great Britain,
Appendix, Vol. II

Source: A.B.T. American Atlas

chief British delegate, observed to T. F. Bayard, President Cleveland's Secretary of State, that demarcation was difficult and expensive. He therefore proposed a conventional line, that is a line by mutual agreement, "on the give and take principle." Canada might lease all or part of the strip in return for Canada's advancing the line to the east, a proposal Chamberlain said Macdonald agreed to. He also suggested that the two experts, Drs. G. M. Dawson and W. H. Dall, should thrash the matter out. Dawson was thereupon summoned to Washington.

Dawson, using the arguments of Justice Gray and Colonel Cameron, did not even convince all the Canadian delegation of his contentions. Sir Charles Tupper and John S. Thompson (later Sir John, Attorney General and later Premier) prevailed in their opinion that the British Columbia line up Clarence Strait was "untenable." In the informal conference between the two experts, Dawson was even less successful in convincing Dall. Repeated re-assertions by the United States of the informality of this conference did not conceal that the United States had heard the Canadian contentions. Dawson maintained that the crest of the mountains observed by Vancouver from the sea and marked on his map constituted the boundary. Dall argued that Vancouver's atlas did not show a continuous row of mountains, but only an indication of a mountainous shore area. Dawson also contended that the heads of the inlets were territorial and hence, according to international law, Canadian waters. Dall also differed with this interpretation: in 1825 Russia had demanded an undivided coastline; and moreover if " 'the heads of all inlets were British territory there was no need of any concession by Russia for her to reach them.' "[15] Beyond recommending the need for settlement the experts failed to agree. Secretary Bayard proposed a survey of the disputed area, as had been proposed in Canada two years earlier.

Yet Canadian authorities were not quite as indifferent to a boundary settlement as their coolness suggested. In October, 1888, the government protested that the preliminary surveys authorized by the United States could not fix the boundary. On being informed of this protest the American Minister E. J. Phelps invited participation. Although Canada was informed of the invitation by the Colonial Office, Lord Salisbury did not pass Canada's acceptance on to the United States Government ostensibly because the Cleveland Government had only four more months of life, but probably because of some indifference to the Canadian claims and almost certainly because of his anger at the dismissal in 1888 of Sir Lionel Sackville-West from his post as British Minister to Washington.[16] Unofficially, however, Canada had been virtually invited to participate in the surveys, but merely replied that the matter was "under consideration."[17] Canada did not co-operate because United States surveys were based on the assumption that the line in the Treaty of 1825 was impractical, an assumption Canada denied. Hence before undertaking a joint survey Canada held that the countries should first come to an agreement that the survey was to delimit the boundary laid down in the Treaty of 1825. Canada did, however, send a man "incognito" to report on the American survey.[18]

Two years later, after Canada had torpedoed United States-Newfoundland reciprocity, and a Canadian-American settlement seemed more urgent, the Alaska boundary question was again discussed but placed last on the list of problems to be considered. Evidently more important matters were on the Canadian Government's mind. Though the boundary settlement continued to grow in importance, in the spring of 1892 at a conference in Washington it was still incidental to the more important reciprocity problem. But Canada could not continue virtually ignoring the boundary question; further delay would harm Canada's interests. Dawson, for example, had learned from the Superintendent of the United States Coast and Geodetic Survey, Thomas D. Mendenhall, that preliminary surveys were being systematically pursued up river valleys and boundary monuments placed thirty miles from tide water, that is, in accordance with the map line. Dawson warned Thompson that such surveys, though not "binding", were "evidently intended to be advanced as a sort of prescriptive claim to territory which, it will probably be stated, we never gave any attention to."[19]

When the boundary question came up at the conference Thompson observed that the vital questions were the interpretation of the treaty and a method of demarcation. The Secretary of State, James G. Blaine, proposed the appointment of a committee to make a settlement and invited a suggestion from the Canadians. Thompson made two proposals: first, a reference to an "impartial authority" to determine the "true boundary"; and secondly, a commission of four experts to decide the mode of demarcation or advise "adoption of a conventional boundary." Blaine countered by proposing a two-year joint survey from Portland Canal to the 141st meridian. On completion the two governments might then "establish the boundary" according to the "spirit and intent of the existing treaties." Thompson accepted this American counter-proposal.[20]

A treaty was drafted and approved. By March, 1893, both sides had appointed their commissioners: the United States, Thomas B. Mendenhall, and Canada, W. F. King; and they and their staffs gathered topographical data for most of the Panhandle area. On the last day of December, 1895, the two commissioners presented a joint report and maps to the two governments at the height of the Venezuela Crisis.[21]

Chapter III

Canada's National Challenge
to the Map Line 1896-1899

Except in British Columbia the Alaska boundary dispute had hitherto been a matter of diplomacy. Why did an essentially provincial interest become a national interest — a symbol of Canada's ambition and frustration?

The Venezuela Incident of 1895-96 marked the beginning of the transformation. The demand of the United States that the Venezuela-British Guiana boundary be submitted to arbitration brought Great Britain and the United States to the verge of war. Had it come Canada would have been the chief battleground. The incident also exposed the hostility of President Cleveland's administration to Canada for it had contended that it was "unnatural and inexpedient" for a country in America to belong to a European country. Six months later a plank in the platform of the victorious Republican party called for Canada's annexation, if the Dominion desired it. Canadians repressed this affront to their country's independence and the implications of Britain's surrender to a forced arbitration.

But resentment expressed itself against the aggressiveness of the United States economic policy, for Canada's confidence in its future came back with the return of prosperity in 1897. The new Premier, Wilfrid Laurier, made overtures of economic conciliation. They were met with rebuff in the Dingley Tariff of 1897, which was the highest American tariff up to that time. An angry Canadian public opinion forced the Laurier Government to pass laws of retaliation. By means of laxity or nonenforcement the government reduced these laws to gestures of

33

retaliation. In effect the preference on British goods was also an anti-American gesture. But the unexpected popularity of Imperial Preference, as it came to be called, followed by Laurier's triumphant visit to England in 1897 for the Diamond Jubilee and the Colonial Conference, awakened the government to the political value of Imperial policies, that is, of orienting Canadian policies towards Britain. Accordingly until the outbreak of the Boer War the Canadian Government in response to an increasing anti-Americanism pursued policies tending to be less national and more imperial. It must be emphasized, however, that anti-Americanism among Canadians was not hostility to individual Americans, with whom great friendliness has always existed, but to their collective personality, aggressive ideology, and national policy. To Canada in the era 1897-99 the most provocative and frustrating American policy was the ability of the United States to maintain the "open door" in the Yukon Gold Rush and its boundary contentions in the Panhandle.[1]

THE OPEN DOOR IN THE YUKON AND THE NEED FOR A BOUNDARY SETTLEMENT

When news of spectacular gold discoveries reached Seattle in July, 1897, thousands of miners from all over the world set out for the Klondike in the Yukon. To reach the Klondike required an incredibly difficult journey. Prospectors had to sail past the treacherous Alaskan coast to the mushroom cities of Dyea and Skagway (an Indian name said to mean "cruel wind") at the end of the Lynn Canal — the most convenient place of access. From Dyea they climbed to the Chilkoot Pass — in places at an angle of more than 45° (see picture on p. 35)[2] or from Skagway to the White Pass, whence they proceeded to Lake Bennett. Here prospectors gathered to build boats in sub-arctic winter or arranged transportation in order to sail down a treacherous river to Dawson City in the heart of the goldfields.

Spectacular fortunes could be made in the Yukon bonanza, but most of them were made by Americans and not Canadians. American success was not simply that most miners were Americans and that they possessed more wealth and experience and

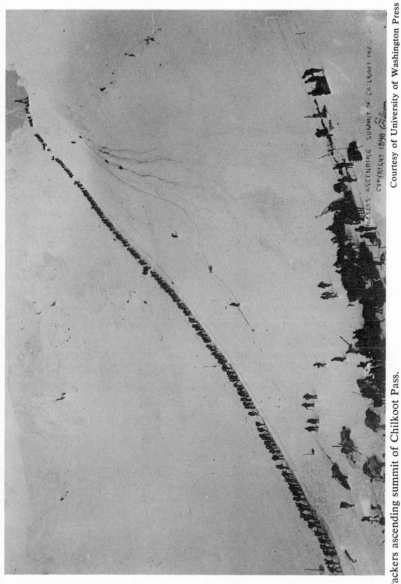

Packers ascending summit of Chilkoot Pass.

the will and the skill but also that the United States could ensure economic equality for its citizens because of political control of the Panhandle. Thus the United States could deny Canada the benefit of Yukon sovereignty by being able to enforce a policy of the "open door."[3]

Furthermore, might not the imperialist policy and mood of the United States exhibited in the Venezuela Incident, and soon to be flaunted in the Spanish-American War and in the annexation of Hawaii, have led to the seizure of the Yukon. Border scuffles early in 1898 on the whereabouts of the Alaska boundary suggested that ominous possibility. An alarmed Canadian Government reinforced the police and made difficulties for the American Relief Expedition, which had been authorized by Congress and organized by the United States War Department because of a rumoured famine in the Yukon and Alaska. In April, when the famine was proved to be a rumour, the United States abandoned the expedition. In the meantime in March to reinforce the police further and to prevent lawless miners making the Yukon "another Texas," the Canadian Government also authorized the dispatch of the Yukon Field Force of 200 men. What primarily saved the Yukon, however, was the United States ability to maintain an open door and British friendship in the Spanish-American dispute.

Most Canadians, however, scarcely thought of guarding against such military or political possibilities. What angered them were the economic advantages that resulted from the United States control of the Panhandle. Expensive mining outfits bought in Canada, for example, had to be transported across the Panhandle either in bond, which required payment of an accompanying convoy fee up to $9.00 per day or payment of American duties. American outfits of course had to pay Canadian duties. But after convoy or duty payments were added to the value of the Canadian outfits, Canada received little economic advantage in selling Canadian mining outfits. Late in 1897 the Minister of the Interior, Clifford Sifton, therefore induced the Secretary of the Treasury, Lyman P. Gage, to reduce or eliminate convoy fees, but they were not removed until May, 1898, and then apparently only half-heartedly.[4]

Could the necessity of payment of American duties or convoy fees be circumvented? The Canadian Government thought so, and hastily let a contract to Mackenzie and Mann railway interests and introduced a bill into Parliament for the so-called "all-Canadian" route to the Yukon. This route lay across the Panhandle up the Stikine River to Telegraph Creek in Canadian territory, whence a narrow-gauge, 150-mile Yukon railway was to be built to Lake Teslin. Here after building a boat a prospector would sail the lake and down the river to the goldfields. But the Canadian Government had not inquired whether the United States would permit transshipment of goods at the mouth of the Stikine River from an ocean to a river vessel. The United States exercised this authority under the Treaty of Washington. Furthermore the Mackenzie and Mann contract contained a five-year monopoly clause excluding railways from the Yukon. In retaliation the United States Senate passed provisions of an act authorizing the Secretary of the Treasury to regulate bonding and transshipment privileges. Although these threats angered the Canadian Government the widespread opposition to the bill in Canada on account of its monopoly provisions helped to defeat the Yukon Railway Bill in the Canadian Senate.[5]

In the meantime the government had sought to mollify the United States. Sifton and Laurier made statements in Parliament in February, 1898, admitting Canada's failure to protest the founding of Dyea and Skagway in 1897 — though they did not disclose that Canada had not even thought of protesting[6] — yet they claimed that the end of the Lynn Canal was "disputed territory," according to a correct interpretation of the Treaty of 1825. In a report to the Cabinet, largely following Colonel Cameron's interpretation, Sifton even argued for Justice Gray's, that is, Sir Charles Bagot's fourth contention: that the line ran up Clarence Strait to Ernest Sound, turned east to the 56th parallel, and thence to the summit of the mountains paralleling the coast, and turned northwesterly until it reached the 141st meridian. As early as January, 1896, the educated Canadian public had learned of this British Columbia claim in an article in the *Canadian Magazine* on "The Alaska Boundary Question," by R. E. Gosnell, the British Columbia Provincial Librarian. Even Colonel Cameron had dismissed Gray's line as unsound, and one of Sifton's staff members thought Sifton's whole argument "utterly untenable and dishonest."[7]

Meanwhile the United States exerted pressure apparently to force the making of a temporary boundary which Canada had first proposed. Early in April, 1898, the officer commanding troops at Dyea officially demanded, apparently on the authority of the Acting Secretary of War, that the Canadian police stop exercising jurisdiction at the summits of the Chilkoot and White Passes and at Lake Lindeman.[8] Canada had proposed a temporary boundary at the Chilkoot summit. The United States agreed, and widened the proposal to include the summits of the White and Chilkat Passes. Canada concurred in the boundary on the summit of the White Pass but not on the Chilkat Pass because that pass exceeded ten leagues from the sea. It was not until October 20, 1899, that Britain and the United States officially agreed to a temporary boundary on all three passes.

THE BOUNDARY QUESTION AT THE JOINT HIGH COMMISSION

Laurier also sought to settle the permanent boundary but he hoped it could be arranged at a conference in conjunction with the settlement of other problems. If Canada could trade advantages it would minimize its weakness in relation to the United States. The United States desire to settle the Bering Sea fur-seal question and its fear of the extinction of the fur seals through catching them in the open sea provided Canada with an opportunity to propose a wider conference on all outstanding problems. In March, 1898, the United States consented, and in May a preliminary conference met to decide on procedure and subjects for discussion.[9]

For Canada the Joint High Commission of 1898-99 marked a considerable constitutional advance over the conference that produced the Treaty of Washington (1871). The British delegates to the 1871 conference in Washington consisted of one Canadian and four Englishmen. In 1898-99 there were four Canadians, including the Canadian Premier, one Newfoundlander, and one Englishman, the leader of the British delegation Lord Herschell. Although Britain refused to appoint the four Canadians — Canada must do so itself, thus emphasizing their Canadian rather than their British status,[10] — yet the Canadian delegates managed to leave Herschell with general oversight of the delegation and to place as much responsibility on him as possible. As for the United States delegation its strength indicated the seriousness of its negotiating intentions. John W. Foster, a former Secretary of State, was the principal American negotiator in charge of the Alaska dispute.

The boundary negotiations began with Canada's advancing the extreme British Columbia claim with an accompanying map (p. 29). This unwise claim, which would have given Canada the heads of the inlets, exposed the Dominion to the subsequent charge of its being a "manufactured" claim. But Herschell argued that in the Treaty of 1825 the word "océan" had replaced the word "mer" (which referred to salt water in general). This replacement implied that the inlets, which were part of the "mer," such as the Lynn Canal, were outside the scope of the treaty.

John W. Foster protested against Canada's claim to the heads of the inlets and against its abrupt presentation. He contended that this was a new claim which would make the American boundary one of disconnected promontaries. It is true that Canada had never officially made a specific claim on the Lynn Canal, but only a general claim to the whole boundary south of Mt. St. Elias. Actually the Canadian claim was only "neglected."[11] Canada had a plausible legal case in its interpretation of the Treaty of 1825, if subsequent interpretation, precedent, and occupation were discounted. On the other hand the United States claim followed the usual map line.

Serious negotiations did not begin until after the Republican electoral victory of November, 1898. After offers and counter-offers the United States consented to a Canadian proposal of a port at Pyramid Harbor. This port was to be under the nominal sovereignty of the United States for as long as Canada maintained customs and police posts at the harbour. In addition Canada offered a general boundary line midway between Canadian and American claims. Unfortunately the proposal leaked out — a leak Herschell hinted that Joseph Chamberlain, the Colonial Secretary, was responsible for[12] — and produced a storm of opposition in the Western states. They objected to the surrender of sovereignty and to the right of Canadian vessels to frequent Lynn Canal harbours reciprocally with American vessels. The American delegation embarrassingly had to withdraw the Pyramid Canal offer.

With an Alaska boundary offer withdrawn both sides knew that the possibilities of compromise were ending. Pressures for agreement were lacking. The United States mood of generosity to Canada on Britain's account was evaporating. In Canada there was national opposition to making any treaty with the United States. Britain, too, had appeared to sacrifice past Canadian interests though Britain's contemporary victory over France in the Fashoda affair appeared to demonstrate that Britain need not do so.

How could Canada break off with the least damage to its internal and external interests? The Alaska boundary question was the internal issue best suited to keep Canada united, but the most dangerous externally. For Canada to use United States failure to agree to an Alaska boundary as an excuse to break off negotiations was to break off where Canada's diplomatic position was weakest and the United States strongest. The United States began to assume that it had nothing essential to arbitrate. The United States was also angry because Canada refused to conclude a treaty on most of the other twelve matters discussed on which they had virtually agreed.

Diplomatic compromise having failed, the reluctant alternative was arbitration, which Britain suggested and the United States rejected. To the United States arbitration might mean compromising its vital interests. It therefore proposed a commission of inquiry, which Britain rejected as leaving the line undetermined. The United States next proposed an arbitration excluding the Lynn Canal area. But this exclusion would make arbitration meaningless to Canada. As an inducement for the United States to agree to arbitration the British Cabinet now offered to abrogate the Clayton-Bulwer Treaty (1850). Under this treaty both Britain and the United States agreed to cooperate if a canal across the Central American isthmus was constructed and to refrain from fortifying or maintaining exclusive control over the canal. The United States wanted the Clayton-Bulwer Treaty abrogated but not at the price of offering concessions in Alaska. The United States was also embarrassed at the British demand for arbitration on the Venezuelan model, that is, an uneven numbered tribunal with a neutral umpire. Less than three years earlier it had imposed that type of arbitration on Britain and Venezuela.

The breakdown of the Joint High Commission turned on the nature of the tribunal and the subjects for arbitration. Britain proposed a tribunal with a neutral European umpire and the United States with a South American umpire. Britain opposed a South American umpire as inexperienced and the United States, a European umpire as ignorant of American customs. Britain also proposed that Pyramid Harbor be explicitly designated as belonging to Canada in answer to the United States designation of Dyea and Skagway as belonging to the United States. As neither side would consent to these conditions the United States proposed an arbitral commission of six, three on a side, the majority deciding, and with Dyea and Skagway as American. Herschell turned this proposal down: an even-numbered commission might be deadlocked, and thus prolong a dangerous boundary problem. Under the United States proposal it could not lose and might win; and it was the proposal essentially adopted in 1903. And so the Joint High Commission ostensibly adjourned but in reality broke down in complete failure.[13]

The United States blamed Herschell for the Commission's lack of progress, but after its breakdown discerned Canada's responsibility. The fact was Canadians were in an angry jingo mood, for which there was considerable justification: the United States had threatened Canada politically and economically, and was using its power and geographic position to force Canada to share in the fruits of the Dominion's Yukon bonanza. But in aping Uncle Sam without his resources or power or will Jack Canuck was playing a dangerous adolescent game. By asserting a quasi-autonomous role in virtually summoning and disbanding the Joint High Commission when problems other than the Alaska one had been practically agreed upon, Canada was going to be held for irresponsibility. Laurier naively believed that Canada could obtain a treaty whenever he wanted. In fact he had let the best time slip by because the United States could afford to wait.

ANTI-AMERICANISM AND PROVISIONAL AND
PERMANENT BOUNDARY NEGOTIATIONS

Canadians regarded the failure of the Joint High Commission in 1899 as a victory for Canada — an expression of jingo defiance. It was a signal for the outbreak of an anti-American press campaign and a call for retaliation by Sir Charles Tupper, the Leader of the Opposition. Americans noticed this journalistic anti-Americanism, and contemptuously replied in kind. The Canadian Government did not yield to the anti-American clamour, but the Ontario and British Columbia Governments did. To force Congress to repeal a lumber provision of the Ding-

Sir Wilfrid Laurier   Courtesy of Public Archives of Canada

ley Tariff, which threatened an additional duty on lumber if a foreign export duty were imposed, the Ontario legislature in 1898 passed a law requiring the manufacture of logs into timber before export to the United States. The British Columbia legislature passed a mining law requiring alien miners to become British subjects, a law eventually declared beyond its powers.

Thus Laurier in 1899 had to cater to a vehement anti-Americanism and enthusiasm for Imperial unity, both of which continued to intensify until the outbreak of the Boer War. In July, for example, when British Columbia's anti-Japanese acts were disallowed, Laurier justified disallowance on grounds of Imperial necessity: if Canada took the "glory and the advantages" of "our Imperial connection . . . we must also take the duties," an assertion that evoked lengthy parliamentary cheering.[14] So powerful was the mood of Imperial unity that the Canadian Parliament approved the construction of a Pacific Cable from Vancouver to Australia, in which Canada had only a slight material interest. Moreover in response to Chamberlain's inquiry whether Canada would take part in a South African military demonstration and in response to public pressure from Britain and Canada for a resolution supporting Britain's South African position, Laurier on July 31 introduced such a resolution. Parliament passed it unanimously, to the patriotic singing of "God Save the Queen."[15]

The mood in Canada that was making Canada and Britain imperially one was largely the result of anti-Americanism. When Sir Charles Tupper on July 22, 1899, placed the Conservative party behind the Liberal Government on Alaska boundary matters, this feeling intensified. Tupper also thundered out against the United States in its determination to keep Dyea and Skagway. It was a "monstrous" and "insulting proposition" to Canada. He also warned of Britain's tendency to give way to the United States.[16]

Canada's diplomatic rigidity that resulted from this jingo mood made Canada an easy prey for Secretary of State John Hay's astute diplomatic suavity and firmness. After the breakdown of the Joint High Commission the United States made the first diplomatic move by hinting that Canada reconvene the Commission. Laurier refused: he considered that the United States should make the first move, and later required acceptance of the Venezuela precedent as a condition. Hay also tried to arrange a temporary boundary on the Chilkat Pass, particularly at Porcupine Creek, where some 3,000 American miners had poured in, many to escape British Columbia's naturalization law. Rumours of Canadian police encroachments prompted an order on May 5, 1899, to dispatch United States troops to Pyramid Harbor. On Britain's immediate protest, this order was countermanded.

Meanwhile in mid-May the American Ambassador to Britain, Joseph A. Choate, and Sir Julian Pauncefote, the British Ambassador to the United States, on his way as a British delegate to the Hague Peace Conference, proposed an odd-numbered tribunal of seven, the seventh member to be chosen by the three British and three American members. "Settled districts," that is, Dyea and Skagway, were to be guaranteed to the United States. Only on condition that Canada was guaranteed Pyramid Harbor, which Canada had never even settled or occupied, would it approve the odd-numbered tribunal.

Canada's rejection of the scheme, which angered Britain and the United States, though Canada had never been consulted, produced three approaches to a boundary settlement. The first was Hay's angry cable to Choate imperatively demanding a *modus vivendi* — a temporary boundary agreement. Hay agreed to the junction of the Chilkat and Klehini Rivers, proposed by Canada the year before, with a line running along the Klehini River. He balked at the "stupid" policy of including Porcupine Creek in Canadian territory, and countered with a line north of the Klehini River. On receipt of the counter-proposal Chamberlain exploded and threatened to break off negotiations. Accordingly Hay drew the line along the Klehini River excluding the Porcupine Creek area from the Canadian claim. Thus early in August, 1899, the temporary boundary in the Chilkat Pass area was decided upon though Canada continued to haggle over details.[17]

Canada's rejection of the odd-numbered tribunal also changed Chamberlain's attitude. Hitherto he was inclined to encourage Canada as Lord Herschell had done, but now his sympathies hardened. He called for a Colonial Office analysis of the Canadian claim. John Anderson's analysis of June 9, 1899, demonstrated how weak Canada's claim in the Lynn Canal was:

Canada's failure to protest the founding of Dyea and Skagway, the establishment of a Canadian custom's post beyond the American claim, and the attempt to build an "all-Canadian" route indicated Canada's acceptance of possession by the United States of the Lynn Canal. Chamberlain therefore requested, and had to keep badgering, Canada to send an expert to Britain to "dispute United States claim founded on occupation and settlement and tacit acquiescence in their interpretation of the Treaty of 1825."[18]

In July a second approach was the revival of a scheme not unlike one that had foundered at the Joint High Commission. The scheme called for Canada to accept a perpetual lease of half a square mile for handling goods at Pyramid Harbor, which was to be connected with the interior by a railway. The American administration approved the scheme because a lease implied United States possession. That was precisely why Canada disapproved; a lease would prohibit an exclusively Canadian carrying trade.

Chamberlain was very angry at this disregard of diplomatic reality. With the approval of the Foreign Office, the Prime Minister, and the Cabinet he cabled Canada a stiff warning:

> We desire to impress upon your Ministers that whatever arguments may be based on letter of Treaty of 1825, careful examination of United States case for possession of shores of Canal based on continuous uninterrupted jurisdiction since the date of Treaty, and admissions of Hudson [sic] Bay Company, Imperial and Dominion governments, shows that it is unassailable. Delay in settlement highly prejudicial to Canadian interests . . .

No one could deny the logic of his warning nor could a Canadian leader ignore the certainty of angry opposition of the Canadian public had the proposal of a lease become known. Twice Britain had been embarrassed through failure to consult Canada first. Canada was emerging from colonialism to nationhood, and though the Dominion had to be consulted it also had to learn that it could not ignore diplomatic reality.[19]

The third approach was to begin diplomatic negotiations for the settlement of the whole boundary. Lord Salisbury began on

July 1, 1899, by proposing to Ambassador Choate an arbitration modelled after the Great Britain-Venezuela arbitration which had been "adopted . . . largely at the instance of, the United States" and because the Alaskan and Venezuelan questions were essentially similar. Choate, aware that Britain thought the Canadian claim weak, on August 9, 1899, denied the similarity and described the terms of the Venezuela treaty as "wholly inapplicable": the Venezuela question had been disputed for more than half a century; the Alaska boundary question only recently. Moreover the American case was based on unprotested map claims, possession, and occupancy of Alaska.

Lord Salisbury replied on October 14. Responding to Choate's implication of the manufactured nature of the Canadian case, Salisbury replied that the whole boundary was in dispute and that Britain had laid claim to Lynn Canal in 1888. The United States therefore occupied undetermined territory, and its sovereignty had only been exercised in that region very recently. The real issue, Salisbury emphasized, was referral of the boundary question to a tribunal essentially like the Venezuela Tribunal.[20] This phase of the diplomatic argument for a permanent boundary came to a virtual end with Choate's reply of January 22, 1900. It was essentially a reaffirmation and development of the arguments in his August 9, 1899 dispatch.

While permanent boundary negotiations were making no progress, Canadians continued to be blinded by the prospect of boundary success. This national illusion was the result of confidence in prosperity and resentful anti-Americanism, largely masked by enthusiasm for Imperial unity, not unlike the two sides of a coin — a coin of jingoistic emotion. It was very difficult to free Canadians from their illusions because Laurier himself had led Canada into the Joint High Commission and broken off on United States failure to agree to Canada's contentions. That is, he bore considerable responsibility for Canada's state of mind. Furthermore, the support of the Conservative Opposition for the Government's Alaska policy restricted its manoeuvrability and made Laurier even more a prisoner of a national policy.

But a dangerous unsettled boundary could not continue un-

IF THE SMALL PERSON IS NOT RESTRAINED THE EAGLE MAY LOSE HIS TEMPER.
—From the *Herald* (New York).

resolved for ever. American diplomatists were angry. Hay
called Canada a " 'spoiled child' . . . unsetting the American
apple cart."[21] The Canadian case was weakened by its badness,
by the increasingly unwillingness and inability of Britain to
render it support, and by United States insistence on its resolution.

Chapter IV

The Boer War and the
Alaska Boundary Dispute 1899-1902

The Boer War had decisive effects on the outcome of the Alaska boundary dispute. It increased Canadian expectations of British help but it weakened the conditions under which Canada's boundary aspirations had grown and thrived. The widening gulf between aspiration and reality could only result in catastrophe for Canada.

CANADA'S BOUNDARY POSITION WEAKENS

The expectation of continued British help was implicit in the movement for Imperial unity, of which participation in war was its military fulfilment. Canada's need for help became obvious in the summer of 1899 when the Dominion took an adamant stand for its boundary contentions against the United States. Thus Canada's participation in the Boer War on October 14, 1899, was largely inspired by an underlying fear of United States anger at those contentions. This fear does not deny the more obvious contemporary motives for participation, such as jingoism, Anglo-Saxon racialism, lust for adventure, and the like, nor the more permanent motives common in World Wars I and II — loyalty to the monarch, British institutions, traditions, and culture. Furthermore during the war itself Britain's frequent expressions of gratitude for Canada's help not only seemed to prove the existence of a tacit Anglo-Canadian alliance, but also widened the popular expectation of continued British support of Canada's boundary claim. In 1902 President Roosevelt recognized that Canadians in send-

48

ing a contingent to South Africa "were demanding a *quid pro quo* which the English were anxious to give."[1]

But expectation of British support was belied by two events. The first was a consequence of Canada's official participation in the Boer War. Britain, delighted with Canada's participation, could now cease to "indulge" Canada's "tendencies,"[2] that is, cease supporting its unrealistic boundary contentions and try to convince Canada of their unreality. Accordingly when the Canadian expert — Sir Louis Davies — and his assistants at last arrived in Britain on September 15, 1899, he presented the Colonial Office with a memorandum of the Canadian case written by Joseph Pope. The memorandum was primarily an attempt to clarify obscurities and apply principles of international law to the interpretation of the Treaty of 1825. It also tried to answer American refutations of Canadian claims. But it could only blandly admit that the Canadian case "was complicated to some extent by the claim of the United States based on alleged prescriptive rights . . . by reason of undisturbed occupation, particularly at the end of the Lynn Canal." It asserted that maps as evidence were unreliable and closed with a ritualistic demand for arbitration on the Venezuela model.[3]

A Colonial Office printed memorandum, almost certainly written by John Anderson, was probably an answer to the Canadian memorandum. It argued that the Canadian case depended on whether Lynn Canal was part of the coast. During the 1825 treaty negotiations the Russian and the British negotiators assumed that the line went around the heads of the inlets. Under the treaty Canada and Britain had a strong case but "subsequent events have seriously impaired it." The maps and the Hudson's Bay Company lease and its termination were "difficult to get over. Still more difficult . . . to explain away" was Britain's failure to protest the map line or the exercise of United States jurisdiction in Alaska. "Our contention has all the appearance of an after-thought . . . For over 60 years we, as well as the other side, accept one interpretation of the treaty, and then we turn around and say 'We have been wrong all the time, and we are entitled to a great deal more than we hitherto thought.' " An arbitrator would not likely listen to that kind of argument.[4]

Meanwhile in September the Colonial Office had made to the Canadians one more arbitration proposal: areas settled in the Lynn Canal before March, 1898, would remain under existing jurisdiction and the losing side would receive compensation. Canada rejected the proposal: it would receive no real equivalent to Dyea and Skagway. As Canada had rebuffed a similar proposal about four months earlier, it would appear that Chamberlain was looking for an excuse to warn Canada officially of some diplomatic facts of life, and Canada's participation in war was the appropriate time. Chamberlain addressed Canada an official dispatch on its rejection of the Colonial Office proposal. He requested Sir Louis Davies to read over the dispatch before being sent to Canada and make suggestions. Davies complained to Anderson that it was "such a knock-down blow to us" that he could scarcely improve upon it. The dispatch defended past British policies and emphasized Canada's failure to protest the founding of Dyea and Skagway. But if an arbitrator did award the two towns to Canada the "transfer could not be peaceably effected," a reference Sir Louis Davies disliked but the truth of which he admitted. It also recommended the advantages of a peaceful settlement, and closed with a recognition of the Canadian Government's responsibility to its people and Britain's promise to continue assisting Canada.

What was this dispatch of November 1, 1899, containing so little that was new and unusually marked "Very Confidential," warning Canada?[5] Its last sentence carried the warning implication: there was a limit to Imperial unity. Britain, too, had a responsibility to its public opinion and to its national interests; Britain would not continue supporting unreasonable boundary contentions.

Laurier could not have missed or misunderstood this warning. It came shortly on the heels of the second event — Canada's defeat in the *modus vivendi* of October 20, 1899, which excluded Canada from a port on the Lynn Canal. Thus Laurier had an object lesson in Britain's refusal — or did it seem inability — to maintain Canada's claim in the Chilkat Pass area. Moreover the agreement of October 20, 1899, was an unmistakable warning that the United States would remain unyielding in the defence of its rights. Unfortunately for Canada, although Laurier would have known that the *modus vivendi* was a defeat

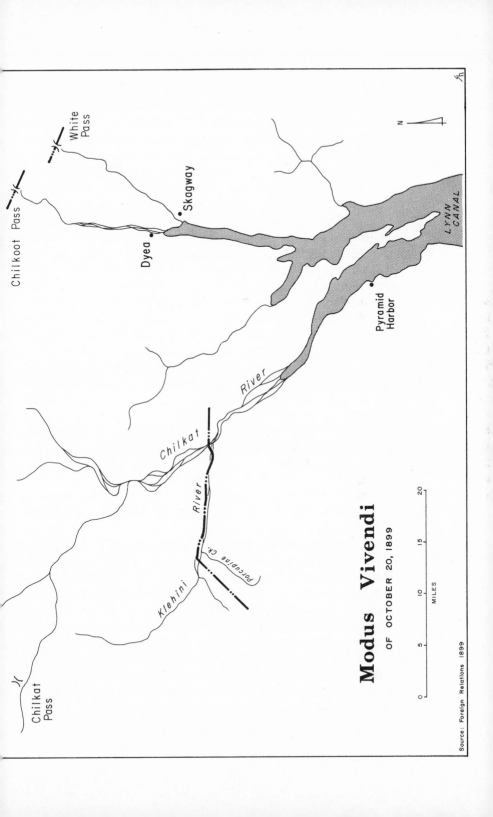

Modus Vivendi

OF OCTOBER 20, 1899

Source: Foreign Relations 1899

the Canadian public did not. The attention of English Canadians especially was caught up in enthusiasm for the Boer War and animosity against French Canadians who opposed participation. They continued to harbour expectations of continued British help.

Apart from the badness of Canada's case and the hints as to Britain's future refusal to give help, Canada's expectations of future British help were belied by Britain's inability to help. The Boer War exposed the decline of Britain's power and shattered its prestige. That the foundations of the *Pax Britannica* were crumbling was already evident in the mid-nineties. By that time Britain was increasingly unable to maintain its position against nationalist and imperialist challenges throughout the world: in the Mediterranean area and in central and eastern Asia; and in America in 1895-6 where Britain had had to yield to the United States; and in Africa two weeks later where Brtain's strategic weaknesses were exposed by the failure of the Jameson Raid and the Kaiser's provocative support of the Transvaal.

The methods adopted to shore up the crumbling foundations of the British Empire begun in the 1870s were failing. Britain had attempted with increasing difficulties in the 1880s to build up a two-power naval standard against the navies of Russia and France. But in relation to the combined navies of United States, Germany, and Japan as well, each of which engaged in huge naval building programmes in the late 1890s, the "two-power standard" was becoming meaningless. Nor since 1870 were the expansion and consolidation of the British Empire relatively any more successful. The Boer War, which was the climax to British Imperial policies, weakened Britain's power and offered rivals opportunities of expansion and even the possibility of intervention. In July, 1901, Arthur Balfour, successor in 1902 to his uncle Lord Salisbury as Britain's Prime Minister, was reported to have lamented that "for all practical purposes" Britain was "only a third-rate power."[6]

This was an exaggeration because, in spite of the threat of European intervention, the defeats in "Black Week," and the two years of chasing guerillas around South Africa, Britain was not defeated. Britain won because of its strength and will, and the support of the United States and German Governments, and partly of the American, but not of the German, people. In other words, Britain's next answer to her relative decline was the cultivation of friends and allies. Of these the United States was most important. Indeed the unofficial Anglo-American entente dating from the Spanish-American War was essential for the maintenance of Britain's power.[7]

United States support of Britain's interests in the Boer War did not mean neglect of American strategic and naval interests, especially for an Isthmian Canal through Nicaragua or Panama. The Spanish-American War had shown the American public the strategic necessity of a canal and provoked a widespread desire to ride roughshod over Britain's rights in the Clayton-Bulwer Treaty. Hay and Pauncefote had drafted an amended version of that canal treaty in January, 1899, but Britain's demands for the exchange of British canal rights for American boundary concessions in Alaska brought about a collapse of negotiations. By the next Congressional session in December, 1899, American pressure to build a canal regardless of the unpopular Clayton-Bulwer Treaty forced Hay and Pauncefote in January, 1900, to resurrect the moribund treaty. It provided for sole United States construction of a canal, its neutrality, openness to the ships of all nations in war and peace, absence of fortifications, and an invitation to other nations to adhere to its terms.[8]

Chamberlain sought Canada's approval. While promising continued support for Canada's Alaska boundary interests, and gratified with Canada's assistance in the Boer War, Chamberlain argued that if the Pauncefote treaty was not approved the bill for the construction of a canal would pass Congress. Canada yielded quickly, but ritualistically pleaded once more for a Venezuela-type arbitration of the unsettled boundary.[9] In 1902 Laurier stated in Parliament that Canada had no direct interest in the abrogation of the Clayton-Bulwer Treaty.

In spite of Britain's surrender of valuable rights the proposed canal treaty met strong opposition from rival transportation interests, supporters of the Monroe Doctrine, and senators piqued at failure to be consulted by Hay. Widespread anti-English sentiment during the election year of 1900 also called for the postponement of the treaty by the Senate until after the election. Despite President McKinley's resounding re-election the campaign disclosed a growing demand for an American-built and American-controlled Isthmian Canal. To head off this possibility the canal treaty was re-introduced into the Senate. The Senate mangled it out of recognition: it supported an amendment permitting fortification, omitted the section requiring adherence of other powers, and abrogated the Clayton-Bulwer Treaty in an incidental fashion. Instead of exercising his veto, the President forwarded the mangled treaty to Great Britain.[10]

Britain was angry and, though aware that she could not stop United States construction of the canal nor afford United States hostility, rejected the amended treaty in the hope of better terms. Since approval of an appropriate canal treaty was certain Hay and Pauncefote simultaneously produced drafts of three treaties: the first on the Isthmian Canal, the second on the Alaska boundary, and the third on most of the outstanding political problems considered in the Joint High Commission of 1898-99. The new canal treaty dignified the abrogation of the Clayton-Bulwer Treaty with a separate article, provided for United States construction and control of a canal, placed the question of neutrality under the authority of the United States, and omitted consideration of the defence of the canal. In December, 1901, the treaty was overwhelmingly approved by the United States Senate.[11] Though Britain had had to give way all her rights in the Clayton-Bulwer Treaty this was the price of retention of American friendship.

The bearing of the canal treaty on the Alaska treaty, however, will be best understood after consideration of the unsettled boundary from 1899-1902.

UNITED STATES HARASSMENT OF CANADA IN THE BOUNDARY AREA 1899-1902

While the United States Administration was cautious not to embarrass Britain on Boer War matters, on Alaska boundary questions it did not hesitate to harass Canada. It probably did so as pressure for a settlement. The Canadian public entranced or repulsed by the Boer War and agitated by racial conflict scarcely noticed the five modes of harassment. Indeed the boundary question now reverted to a local and diplomatic dispute.

In the first place under the *modus vivendi* of October 20, 1899, neither Indians nor miners were to "suffer . . . diminution of the rights and privileges which they now enjoy." Under this provision Indians demanded and obtained with United States support virtually free-trade privileges in the Chilkat area. Nor could Canada resist United States intervention on behalf of American miners who particularly disliked the prospect of being forced to become British subjects under British Columbia law. Despite the law's being declared *ultra vires,* miners and West Coast interests petitioned President McKinley against the *modus vivendi.* Not only had Secretary Hay to defend his diplomatic victory in the *modus vivendi,* but he also promised to safeguard miners' rights. "The rights of the United States in the matter of the Treaty boundary are absolutely intact and their assertion in due time will be earnest and thorough." Apparently Canadian officials did not notice this emphatic warning; and after the Tribunal decision Laurier complained bitterly of American territory extending twenty miles beyond the temporary boundary in the Chilkat area.[12]

A second method of harassment, which had begun in 1899, was denial of legal rights to Canadian miners in Alaska. Under Section 13 of the Alaska Homestead Act of 1899 a Canadian miner was to enjoy the same mining privileges in Alaska as Americans, provided American miners enjoyed the same mining privileges as Canadians in the Yukon. American miners did enjoy the same leasing privileges as Canadian miners did in the Yukon. But on the technicality that leasing a claim was not the same as owning one — the American practice in Alaska — Canadians were denied the right to own claims in Alaska. Although the Canadian Government might complain about this "flimsy and questionable" pretext, the Colonial Office realized that any protest to the United States would be futile.[13]

A third type of harassment — this time of presumed Canadian sovereignty — was the appearance on a United States Geodetic Survey map of marks indicating four United States Government storehouses on Wales and Pearse Islands in Portland Inlet. In October, 1901, the Canadian Government protested their presence, though they had been erected in 1896.[14]

Prior to their appearance on a map the Canadian Government apparently chose to ignore their existence. They were now becoming important because the Canadian Government, having been defeated in the *modus vivendi* to a claim on the Lynn Canal, was shifting its interest to the Portland Inlet.

A fourth type of harassment, which had continued since the beginning of the Yukon Gold Rush, concerned difficulties in the transportation of goods to the Yukon. Shortly after the outbreak of the Boer War, Canadian Pacific Railway ships lost the privilege of conveying American goods in bond from American ports and touching at Canadian ports before landing goods at Skagway. American ships, it was argued, could now fulfil the demands of transport.[15] Moreover American customs officials speeded American goods to their destination but often delayed passage of Canadian goods, by tardy and thorough inspection, etc.

A fifth type of harassment concerned the conveyance of prisoners. For example, in response to a Canadian request for permission to convey an accused murderer across the Panhandle, Hay in effect replied that the President could not guarantee that a writ of *habeas corpus* would not be issued to free the prisoner. He artfully reminded Canada that the question of the conveyance of prisoners had been discussed at the Joint High Commission. The Canadian Government later vainly sputtered that the United States should not be allowed "to exercise unquestioned, the privilege [of conveying prisoners] which is denied Canada."[16]

These and other inconveniences fell on the North-West Mounted Police. A memorandum complained:

> Unpleasantness frequently occurs through misunderstanding or overzeal on the part of the U.S. officials in asserting jurisdiction, and conditions are made as disagreeable as possible for Canadian Officials. There have been one or two narrow escapes from international complications through the placing of the flags of the United States or Canada.
>
> Smuggling is rampant on the short stretch of the White Pass Railway and, . . . causes a great deal of bitterness.[17]

The reference to the flags refers to rumours in June, 1901, that the British planned to seize Skagway, the signal for which was to be the hoisting of the Union Jack over the White Pass and Yukon railway offices. It also refers to an excitable American who cut down the customs flag over the Canadian customs offices. After an American apology and mutual agreement not to fly customs flags in each others' territory the matter was closed. Five months later in November, 1901, rumours reached an alarmed Ottawa and London of a conspiracy to overthrow the Yukon Government. It was an attempt to bring the frontier question before the American public. Premature disclosure and prompt countermeasures on both sides brought about its collapse.[18]

Thus Laurier could not forget the incessant harassment nor the disparity of power between Canada and the United States. "We are the small dog engaged in a fight with the big dog," he wrote to a Western Member of Parliament.[19] Meantime the United States, however, sent him through the usual diplomatic channels draft treaties on the boundary and on other political problems.

THE HAY-PAUNCEFOTE DRAFT ARBITRATION CONVENTION, MAY, 1901

This draft treaty had its origin in Hay's continuing efforts to effect a permanent boundary settlement. In February, 1900, when Lord Salisbury heard of the possibility of an even-numbered tribunal he urged Pauncefote to do his utmost to establish such a tribunal. One method of doing so was to reconvene the Joint High Commission. Its sole purpose of meeting would have been to consider an arbitration treaty modelled after the territorial provisions of the Olney-Pauncefote Treaty of 1897. That treaty provided for a panel of six arbitrators, three chosen on a side and five out of six to make the decision. Although the unfavourable 1900 election atmosphere and the drastic amendments to the canal treaty militated against success, useful discussions had taken place for the making of the Alaska Draft Arbitration Convention of May, 1901. This treaty called for an "arbitral tribunal . . . of six impartial jurists of repute," three

Lord Minto

chosen by each power, and a majority to decide. It was to determine essentially two questions: (1) Where did the boundary line run in the Portland Inlet? and (2) Was the coastal strip unbroken?[20]

In typically extremist style Chamberlain and Minto tried to rush Laurier into acceptance of the boundary treaty and the treaty on other political problems. Chamberlain argued that Dyea and Skagway were no longer exempted from consideration by the tribunal and the two treaties together with the canal treaty might all be considered together. Within ten days an adamant "no" on the Alaska treaty and indifference to the other treaty came from Canada. This answer made the Colonial Office, the Foreign Office, and the State Department angry. Laurier explained to Minto that the Dyea and Skagway concession was meaningless since the American proposal was to determine not where British territory touched the sea but its distance therefrom. Nor had the United States made any concession in the Clayton-Bulwer Treaty. Two weeks later, however, Canada hinted vaguely at re-considering "the possibility of a Court as at present proposed." Once more Chamberlain held out the possibility of an exchange of concessions in the canal treaty for concessions on the Alaska boundary though in the year before he had confessed there was not a "ghost of a chance" of such an exchange. When the Senate approved the canal treaty on December 16, 1901, even that ghostly possibility vanished.[21]

In mid-October Canada made a third reply. It agreed to the appointment of an even-numbered tribunal — three on a side, with the third member on each side chosen from genuinely neutral countries. It also suggested alternative questions of reference: six questions allowing for the Canadian interpretation and not two favouring the American interpretation. The six questions concerned (1) the whereabouts of the beginning of the line at the southern end, (2) the location of Portland Canal, (3) the line between the two preceding points, (4) the point where the line struck the 56th parallel, (5) the location of the crest of the mountains that the treaty said paralleled the coast, and (6) the alternative place where the line was to be measured from.[22] Except for the last these were the same questions raised in the Memorandum which the Colonial Office received in September, 1899. In virtually the same form these became the problems of reference in the Hay-Herbert Treaty. The framing of a boundary treaty in stridently pro-American fashion had provoked Canada into angry opposition and elicited alternative proposals not far from what the United States wanted. This tactic, which Hay had successfully used in 1899 against Canada, shows his astuteness as a diplomatist.

Why had Canada taken a decisive step towards the United States position in two months? During the visit to Canada in September and October, 1901, of the Duke of Cornwall and York (the future George V), Chamberlain instructed Minto to arrange a meeting of the Canadian leaders with Sir John Anderson, the Colonial Office representative who accompanied the Duke to Canada. Anderson convinced Laurier and Minto that Canada's Lynn Canal claim was weak and the one near Portland Canal strong. Indeed the Canadian interest in trade with the Yukon had shifted to its possibilities through Port Simpson, a future transcontinental terminus. Both Laurier and Minto thought Canadian opinion might be "appeased" if Canada kept its title to the southern border.[23] While Anderson was in Canada probably the decisive event occurred — the assassination of President McKinley and the accession to the presidency of the impetuous and incalculable Theodore Roosevelt.

THEODORE ROOSEVELT INTENDS TO BE "UGLY" WITH CANADA

The American public saw in President Roosevelt (1858-1919) the man of action, the epitome of Americanism. A superb politician, a master of the legislative process, and a first-rate administrator, he used the prestige and power of his office for a "square deal," to ensure equity among industrialists, farmers, and labourers. Domestically his tenure of office was memorable. Foreigners, however, have recalled his policy of "Speak softly and carry a big stick," though his actions were usually more moderate than his words. Nevertheless he was the forthright nationalist for whom the acquisition and use of power and the maintenance of American prestige were central in his foreign policy. He had supported President Cleveland, for example,

Theodore Roosevelt speaking at Nahant. Lodge to his right on platform.

The Boer War and the Alaska Boundary Dispute 1899-1902 ✤ *61*

during the Venezuela Incident, and desired the annexation of Canada. He was an ardent advocate of the annexation of the Hawaiian Islands and the armed expulsion of Spain from her empire. Such a man was not content to be guided by his Secretary of State as President McKinley had been; he tended to become the maker and director of American foreign policy. His policy, however, did not differ in substance from that of Hay but only in style. Hay's policy was one of the mailed fist in the velvet glove; Roosevelt often took off the glove. As for the Alaska boundary dispute, Roosevelt held that Canada had not a leg to stand on: its claim was less than twenty years old. The United States had nothing to arbitrate; would Canada arbitrate Nova Scotia.[24] Thus Roosevelt needed no encouragement from an exasperated State Department to take strong action against Canada.

In January, 1902, when Ambassador Choate inquired of the President's policy on Alaska, Roosevelt enjoined him to "let sleeping dogs lie." He did not want divisive issues raised with Britain so long as the Boer War dragged on. By the end of February, however, Pauncefote had received the third Canadian response to the draft treaty of the previous May. He passed it on to Hay, who informed Roosevelt. Early in March Secretary Hay and George Smalley, the London *Times* correspondent in the United States, warned Roosevelt of the danger of a miner's uprising if gold were discovered in Alaska. Roosevelt, who would have known about the threat in the previous November, replied at once that he would send in troops and engineers to draw the boundary. Smalley "terribly disturbed" protested that would be "very drastic." Roosevelt retorted, "I mean it to be drastic." Within two weeks, Senator Henry Cabot Lodge, the fire-eating Senator from Massachusetts, who was influential with the President, induced him to dispatch troops quietly into southern Alaska; and on March 27, Elihu Root, the Secretary of War, received orders to do so. In fact, however, there seems to have been only a replacement of troops in Skagway.[25]

Meanwhile Pauncefote informed the Foreign Office of Roosevelt's opinion on the United States claim as "clear and unquestionable" and of the President's reluctance to hazard American territory to arbitration. The President would only agree to a tribunal giving "reasoned opinions," not a decision.[26] A tribunal offering only "reasoned opinions" would have been politically disastrous to Laurier. His government would have had to carry out an unpalatable decision or submit to Roosevelt's drawing the line, whereas by yielding to the decision of an external tribunal Canada could save its face.

Roosevelt had no intention of saving Canada's face, as his decision to use troops, if necessary, signifies. On the contrary he declared his intention to be "ugly" to Canada, an intention he made sure would be reported to Ottawa. His informants included George Smalley, Colonel Gerald Kitson, the British military attaché, who had recently been commandant of Royal Military College, Cecil Spring-Rice, best man at Roosevelt's wedding and later British Ambassador to the United States, and others, each of whom sent or carried reports to Ottawa of the possibility of violence and of the need for an immediate settlement.[27] This intention seems part of Roosevelt's war of nerves against Laurier. But his greatest weapon was the uncertainty of his own impetuous will.

The war of nerves worked, for when Laurier visited London in June, 1902, to attend the Coronation of King Edward VII and the Colonial Conference, which coincided with the end of the war, he was anxious for a settlement. At first he naively hoped for a *modus vivendi* along the whole disputed line to avoid an explicit surrender of territory; but he forgot America's love of legalism. Meanwhile Minto arranged a conference on June 24, 1902, at the Foreign Office with himself, Laurier, Mulock (later Sir William, 1844-1944) and Lansdowne, oddly without the presence of a representative of the Colonial Office. The conference canvassed the boundary situation, saw the impossibility of (genuine) arbitration, noted the fears of miners, and dreaded the possibility of Roosevelt's taking unilateral action. If a new gold field were discovered, for example, the United States might "take the bull by the horns & hoist the American flag." Laurier approved Lansdowne's plan of sounding Choate "privately & unofficially" on Choate's approaching Laurier to discuss a boundary settlement.[28]

When the American Ambassador was approached by the Foreign Secretary, Choate questioned the object of meeting Laurier. He had heard nothing important on boundary matters since his unanswered dispatch of January 22, 1900. Moreover was the time appropriate? The biennial congressional election would take place in the fall of 1902. Lansdowne explained that an answer to Choate's dispatch had been prepared, but it had been superseded by a memorandum prepared in answer to the Hay-Pauncefote draft treaty.[29] Choate, uninformed of these developments and given copies of these documents by Lansdowne, cabled Washington for permission to meet Laurier. Meanwhile, Henry White, the chargé of the American Embassy, who knew of these developments, met with Laurier. Laurier broached the boundary question because of possible border trouble. He also confessed to White that he knew the United States would not leave Skagway, but pleaded that he would like to " 'save his face' " with Canadians by an arbitration. If the decision went in Canada's favour, the United States could not be turned out of Skagway, but Canada would expect compensation.[30]

During Hay's absence from the Department of State, Roosevelt answered Choate's inquiry through an Acting Secretary of State. He gave permission for Choate to see Laurier but added that "the Canadian claim has not a leg to stand on and that compromise is impossible." After receiving White's report of his interview, Roosevelt wrote to Hay that the United States could not compromise, since the Canadian claim was an

> outrage pure and simple . . . The fact that they have set up such an outrageous and indefensible claim and in consequence are likely to be in hot water with their constituents when they back down, does not seem to me to give us any excuse for paying them in money or territory.

Their claim came "dangerously near blackmail." To Choate, however, Laurier hinted a fundamental concession: Canada would accept the American-type tribunal.[31]

Choate's failure to make an affirmative response to Lansdowne's and Laurier's invitation suggested to the Foreign Secretary that the President showed no interest in negotiations on the basis of the Hay-Pauncefote draft treaty of May, 1901, and of the Canadian reply. Therefore, he answered the virtually outmoded Choate dispatch of January 22, 1900, two and a half years before, an answer which Laurier read over. The original answer prepared earlier than the Hay-Pauncefote proposals was now refurbished to suggest that the Canadian position was weakening. Though much of the August 18, 1902, dispatch went over old ground and recommended a tribunal ensuring finality of decision, it also stated that Britain was not "wedded to a particular formula." The language was softened, too. "Impossible" was changed to "difficult," and "must adhere to the view" to "still consider." Indeed on one change Anderson noted "? too strong if we contemplate giving away."[32]

The fact was Laurier and, almost certainly by then, Lansdowne were prepared to give way.

Canada Big-Sticked:
I The Hay-Herbert Treaty 1903

Once Roosevelt had made up his mind to settle the boundary, Laurier had no practical alternative but to yield to American demands. Because of Canada's blindness to political and diplomatic reality the United States could exploit this situation with deadly diplomatic skill: it could make Britain the instrument of Canada's humiliation.

NEGOTIATIONS FOR THE HAY-HERBERT TREATY

On Laurier's return to Canada in October, 1902, he informed the Cabinet of his consent to an even-numbered tribunal. Some of the members of a self-appointed committee of the Cabinet, to whom Laurier had made a promise not to consent to such a tribunal, were prepared to make a "first-class row."[1] But the time was ill chosen. Laurier had just dismissed the high-tariff Joseph Tarte from the Cabinet and he had to go south for his health.

Meanwhile a new British Ambassador had arrived in Washington to fill the place of the deceased Lord Pauncefote. Sir Michael Herbert (1857-1903) was the scion of a distinguished English family, married to the daughter of a New York banker, related to the Vanderbilts, Ogdens, and Astors, and member of the British Embassy in Washington from 1888-1893. Herbert seems to have owed his appointment to his friend Henry White and to Senator H. C. Lodge. Lord Lansdowne reluctantly agreed to the appointment preferring Sir Mortimer Durand, who became Herbert's successor in Washington.[2] Although Herbert had been a successful first secretary in five important embassies he had never before been a minister or ambassador on his own.

Herbert had the reputation of ability, but Professor Alvin C. Gluek's characterization of him as "always credulous, and frequently careless"[3] seems a little harsh, for on many matters his advice to the Foreign Office was good. In the making of the Hay-Herbert Treaty his major blunders were due to his naive idealism and his lack of expert advice on the Alaska question. Herbert therefore had to become his own expert, which in fact often tended to mean reliance on advice in telegrams and dispatches from Lord Minto.[4]

Negotiations for the treaty began in October, 1902, when Secretary Hay informally suggested to Herbert the proposal of the previous March, a tribunal offering "reasoned opinions." Canada mildly concurred provided all aspects of the question be considered, and Herbert added the suggestion that the decision should be final. Roosevelt now consented to the inclusion of these provisions in the treaty. Why Roosevelt now agreed to a "final decision" is unknown. It may be surmised that the Republican congressional victory of November, 1902, strengthened his hand and that, when he put pressure on Britain to submit the debt dispute between Venezuela and the blockading powers to arbitration, he could hardly exempt the United States from a tribunal that would settle, and not simply offer opinions about, the Alaska boundary.

On learning of United States consent the Canadian Government requested details. Hay supplied the specifics by trotting out the hoary draft treaty of May, 1901. Canada had already responded to this treaty with amendments, which the President had rejected. In December, 1902, Herbert submitted the same Canadian amendments to Hay. Hay now accepted them, with one important exception to be discussed below.[5] In proposing the draft treaty again and in effect inviting the same amendments Hay probably intended to mollify the testy Roosevelt. By yielding in apparent generosity to Canada's amendments Roosevelt could save face. By accepting Canada's case — a juridical interpretation of the treaty — Canada's defeat was made even more galling.

On Laurier's return from the south the Cabinet on January 9, 1903, decided to accept the treaty. But on the next day it had second thoughts. It balked at being saddled with responsibility for almost certain defeat. It too trotted out a timeworn proposal for a tribunal of partly independent jurists or the use of the Hague court of arbitration. Meanwhile Laurier informed Minto of the Cabinet's hesitation: the Cabinet protested not because it believed its request would be granted but because an evenly-divided tribunal was regarded "as an unsatisfactory tribunal." But Laurier added, "if Herbert cannot succeed, let him sign the treaty as it is."[6] In the meantime the German destruction of a Venezuelan port was arousing American indignation against Britain as well. "Telegraph reply as soon as possible," the Colonial Office bluntly ordered Minto.

Laurier knew he had no alternative but to compel the Cabinet to approve the treaty. Even so the Cabinet protested to the end against the structure of the proposed tribunal, a protest that would appear in the published record. Hay therefore wearily replied:

> in view of the alterations he had made in regard to terms of reference he had hoped for a spontaneous acceptance of the treaty. . . . He could only repeat what he had often said before, that the form of arbitration proposed was the only one acceptable to the President, and that a treaty involving submission of question to foreign arbitration or to the Hague tribunal would stand no chance of ratification in the United States Senate.

Accordingly on January 24, 1903, Hay and Herbert signed the boundary convention, popularly known as the Hay-Herbert Treaty.[7]

Article I of the treaty called for a tribunal which

> shall consist of six impartial jurists of repute, who shall consider judicially the questions submitted to them, each of whom shall first subscribe an oath that he will impartially consider the arguments and evidence presented to the tribunal, and will decide thereupon according to his true judgment.

And a majority was to decide. Article II provided that the two parties exchange the cases and other evidence within two months of the date of ratification, that within the succeeding two months they both exchange counter cases with evidence — a period which, however, the tribunal might extend — and that within a third two-month period they should exchange written arguments, which could be supported before the tribunal by oral arguments. The article also provided that within thirty days either side could demand a certified copy of a document from the other, and within forty days the original of the document. Article III laid down that the tribunal, in settling the questions set forth in Article IV below, should take into consideration the Treaties of 1825 and 1867, especially Articles III, IV, and V of the Treaty of 1825, each of which was quoted in full. Article III also laid down that the tribunal could take into consideration the action of governments or its representatives showing their interpretation of the location of the boundaries.

Of the seven questions that Article IV said the tribunal was to answer, Question 5 was decisive for the United States position, being practically the same as Question 2 of the Hay-Pauncefote draft treaty of May, 1901. Did Russia under the Treaty of 1825, it asked, have a "continuous fringe, or strip, of coast on the mainland" separating British territory from "bays, ports," etc., "of the Ocean"? If the answer was, yes, Britain was cut off from the sea. If the answer was, no, and if the summit of the mountains exceeded ten leagues distance from the coast, Article 6 asked from what position and in what manner was the width of the lisière to be measured? Article VII asked what "if any exist," a phrase Hay added,[8] probably for Roosevelt's benefit, are "the mountains referred to as situated parallel to the coast?" The first four questions concerning the southern end of the boundary were the same as those in the Canadian dispatch of November, 1901.

Although Lord Minto's observation that the treaty was "sensibly received" in Canada is probably accurate — for now the boundary question had become a national issue again — the *Literary Digest* reported to its American readers that the Canadian press considered the treaty a "surrender," though its precise terms were not known. In particular the *Digest* seized on an example or two of extreme opinion. It quoted "the following straightforward language" from the Toronto *Evening Telegram*:

The United States carries into diplomacy the arts, graces, and appetites which are exhibited by the highway robber in private life . . . Canada had either to fight or be robbed, and Britain has decided that submission to robbery is cheaper than war. Britain is probably right.[9]

Although there was mock gravity in the introductory phrase the *Literary Digest* account would not weaken American support of the President's views.

"IMPARTIAL JURISTS OF REPUTE"

Early in the negotiations for the Hay-Herbert Treaty the question of British appointments had arisen. Laurier had thought the discussion premature though by January 22, 1903, he considered it "a matter of course that the Chief Justice of England should be a member." In cabling this suggestion to Britain Herbert asked if *any* jurists need be Canadian. Lansdowne thought *one* should be; the Colonial Office thought *all* should be.[10]

On the other hand Herbert idealistically pressed for the appointment of Supreme Court justices. In spite of Hay's hints on the reluctance of the justices, Herbert persisted in suggesting such appointments. Hay gave Herbert a broader hint when he informed him that "passage of the treaty by the Senate depends largely on composition of the tribunal. . . ." As late as January 26 Herbert was reporting that the President was considering the appointment of American judges, two of whom "will probably be judges of the United States Supreme Court." In view of Chief Justice Melville W. Fuller's unhappy experience on the Venezuelan Boundary Arbitration tribunal (1899) it looks as if Roosevelt's inquiry of the justices was *pro forma*, for the justices asked — Edward D. White and Oliver Wendell Holmes — turned him down; and Roosevelt declined to accept their suggestions.[11]

The Hay-Herbert Treaty had to overcome three obstacles before passage by the Senate. The first was the presence in the preamble of the word "arbitral" suggesting an outside body determining a United States boundary. Was this fact not known when the treaty was signed on January 24? Thus the treaty as signed gave Canada the illusion of arbitration. But on January 28 Herbert agreed to delete the word "arbitral," a deletion Canada was apparently not informed of. Thus the corrected version of the Hay-Herbert Treaty transformed the tribunal from a body suggestive of arbitration into one purely diplomatic. The stated purpose of this transformation was to mollify the Senate.[12]

Secondly, since the tribunal created under the Hay-Herbert Treaty made the final decision the Senate would demand that the tribunal appointees be staunch defenders of American interests. Thirdly, the Senate and a vocal section of the American public objected to Britain's and Canada's stance in the Alaska boundary question. Furthermore, the widespread animus against making any treaty with Britain was reinforced by Britain's role in the debt-collecting Venezuela blockade. Britain had joined with Germany to blockade, bombard, and land troops in Venezuela. Collaboration with Germany produced a storm of opposition in Britain and America. On February 7 Herbert warned Lansdowne that the intensity of American opposition required Britain to choose between the friendship of Germany or of the United States. Canadians also seized on Britain's role in this affair to blame her and excuse themselves. As the days passed Lansdowne doubted whether the treaty would pass. On February 10 President Roosevelt informed one of the leading German-American opponents of the treaty that the treaty had no chance of passage.[13]

This was propaganda to disarm the opposition, for President Roosevelt and Senator Lodge had laid careful plans to push the treaty through the Senate. A decisive step in the strategy was the appointment of acceptable "impartial jurists of repute." Lodge had been warned by several colleagues that assurances as to the American commissioners would be required before supporting the treaty. Senator Lodge himself was one of the commissioners chosen. In the recent congressional election campaign Lodge had denounced Canada's "manufactured and baseless" claim to American territory. Senator George Turner, a Democratic Senator from the state of Washington, represented a state and an area adamant in opposition to Canada's claim. Elihu Root, Secretary of War, who it was rumoured intended to retire and who did so nearly a year later on February 1, 1904, was not publically committed, except as a member of a committed administration. All three men would be acceptable to the Senate and reflected the views of Roosevelt, who believed, as A. E. Campbell puts it, it was "an enormous concession to provide an opponent with a means of retreating gracefully from an untenable position."[14]

The treaty was introduced during the scheduled speech of a notorious senatorial bore when many of the opponents of the treaty absented themselves from the Senate chamber. Senator Lodge interrupted the speech by moving that the Senate enter executive — that is, secret session — and the Hay-Herbert Treaty was introduced. Having been authorized to do so by the President, Lodge now disclosed the names of the American appointees to the tribunal. Following a prefunctory discussion and a voice vote the treaty was passed. The Senate opponents of the treaty were furious at this "bit of astute Parliamentary practice,"[15] and on the next day demanded re-consideration of the treaty. Their demand was defeated, not by the constitutional requirement of a two-thirds vote, but by a simple majority. Had usual constitutional procedures been followed the treaty could scarcely have been passed. Politically, therefore, Roosevelt's methods and appointments can be justified; and this political fact was widely recognized in the United States and Canada.

But need the appointment of Root, Lodge, and Turner have been so partial, so blatantly offensive to the principle of "impartial jurists of repute," and so brutal in its warning to Canada of the unmistakable intent of the United States? Hay did not think so, for he was "extremely displeased and protested in the strongest way to the President."[16]

ANGLO-CANADIAN RAGE AGAINST THE "IMPARTIAL JURISTS"

Laurier and Minto first greeted the press reports of the appointments as unbelievable. The unbelievable, however, was soon confirmed from London. The adjectives of British and Canadian officials describing the appointments ranged from Lansdowne's "terrible blow" to Laurier's "fatuous" to Minto's description as a "breach of faith" and Canada as a victim of " 'sharp practice.' " The sense of outrage among Canadians was magnified by American press reports snorting in contempt at the "impartial jurists."[17]

Meanwhile in this resentful and apprehensive atmosphere Britain and Canada groped for a response to the American appointments. At first the Foreign Office thought of appointing three mediocrities — county judges or three partisans — but Lord Lansdowne soon dismissed the idea. The Colonial Office angrily hinted that the Chief Justice be not appointed or even that negotiations be broken off. Lansdowne apparently took

MR. BULL (the land agent): "Is there any hother section of Canader as seems to take your heagle eye, Sammy? Don't let your natural modesty prevent your saying so if there is, y' know."
—*The Toronto World.*

Courtesy of the Toronto *Globe and Mail*

JOHN BULL: "Your H'uncle Sammy and I are going to talk over that little dispute of yours and—er —you might just turn that picture to the wall and keep yourself in the background as much as possible."
—*The Toronto Telegram.*

Courtesy of the Toronto *Sun* Syndicate

fright and requested no further Colonial Office communications to Canada without his consent.

The Canadian Government also protested vigorously against the alleged impartiality of the appointments. Two days later it explained further to the Colonial Office that its consent was based on the stipulation of impartiality and "confidential statement" of Herbert's hope for Supreme Court appointments. The Canadian Government expected these considerations to be made "good"; otherwise it was to be "feared the whole situation would require to be reconsidered."[18] In angry ambiguity the Canadian Government temporized, but did not dare break off. In forwarding these cables to the Foreign Office, the Colonial Office commented on the first that Britain should consider breaking off, and on the second, that it agreed with the Canadian Government's views on the matter.[19] Minto also suggested to Ambassador Herbert that the British side should select "a different class of representatives, partisans to meet those of the enemy. . . ." Nor could the Canadian Government face Parliament because "the outspoken remarks of the President himself are generally known here."[20] The receipt of such opinions by Herbert helps one understand why the United States Post Office began to intercept Minto's mail to Herbert and why the telegraph company garbled Minto's coded messages.[21] Although Minto had expressed himself forcefully to Laurier, his advice was moderate: adhere to the treaty and appoint to the tribunal the British Chief Justice and other Canadian high court justices.

Herbert was blamed by Laurier for failing to make a written protest against the appointments and for encouraging expectations of Supreme Court appointments. Herbert had protested verbally against the appointments, and had sounded John Charlton, then in Washington exploring opinion for Laurier, on the advisability of a written protest. Charlton thought it dubious and useless; replacements would probably support the American contentions. Herbert therefore demurred making a written protest, and reported to Minto that Hay was "evidently over-ruled by the President who has got his back up and who asserts that [no one had?] the right to dictate to him" regarding appointments which he thought "in conformity with the treaty." Later he prophesied to Minto that if the tribunal came to a tie Roosevelt would bow to jingo opinion and settle the boundary by force. Yet an ambassador capable of such discernment under difficult circumstances could weep to Minto like a Victorian maiden: he had "a right to be disgusted and disheartened, and my illusions about everyone are, I fear, gone for ever."[22]

Canada's grievance against Herbert is more justified than that against Alverstone or the Foreign Office ratifying the Hay-Herbert Treaty without Canada's consent. Given President Roosevelt's determination to draw the boundary on essentially American terms, would the presence of a strong and discreet British Ambassador in Washington have made any essential difference? Perhaps Canada might have been treated less brutally. But Canada of course could not know of the American pressure to appoint Herbert.

Meanwhile Laurier clutched at straws. Since officially appointments would not be made until after the exchange of ratifications, Laurier was deluded for a time into believing that Senators Lodge and Turner would withdraw as commissioners. Senator Lodge evidently nourished this delusion by feeding Edward Farrer, a prominent Canadian journalist and one of Laurier's ears in Washington, with unfounded hopes.[23] In a "futile" letter Laurier also appealed to Hay against Lodge and Turner, naively pleading that these appointments would make it "extremely difficult to obtain" legislative assent, presumably for tribunal funds, "and not a little humiliating."[24] A month later in a brutally bland letter Hay replied that "if by 'impartial' you understand without opinion on the subject matter in question," such a man could not be found in the United States. "We have appointed three of the most eminent men in the United States, of spotless character." Although the mind boggles at Hay's contemplation of Senator Lodge as a man "of spotless character," yet Hay's private views on Lodge did not differ essentially from Laurier's. At the same time a messenger, sent by Laurier to Hay to protest the appointment of Lodge and Turner, remarked to Hay: "Sir Wilfrid knows, and all of us know, that we have no case."[25] Was this remark made with Laurier's consent? It fits in, however, with his depressed attitude and with the other evidence of those days. Laurier evidently thought he could appease the American Government by pleading guilty. But to Roosevelt, who thought Canada's case against America's just rights an outrage, a plea of guilty would sanction greater punishment for Canada. Yet Laurier knew he must accept the appointments, evidently delaying acceptance in order to convince his angry Cabinet to accept the appointments and perhaps hoping that something might turn up.

Meantime on February 24 the British Cabinet decided that it could not break off nor challenge the names. Austen Chamberlain, the Postmaster-General, pleaded with Lord Lansdowne to

> reason the Canadians into good humour again and not to leave us the odium of choosing, without their assent, three men, a single one of whom, by agreeing with the Americans, would decide the case against Canada and certainly involve us in a charge of having deserted her interests. . . ."[26]

On the next day (February 25) in an important dispatch, written largely by Lansdowne himself, but sent under the signature of the Colonial Office, the Foreign Secretary endeavoured to reason with Canada. The British Government, the cable began, was "as much surprised" at the appointments as the Canadian Government. As the situation was "full of difficulty," the British Government "earnestly" desired the Canadian Government's concurrence. It reminded the government that a refusal to accept such prominent men would be resented both by the United States Government and the American people. It would probably

> produce lasting ill-will between the two countries. His Majesty's Government are, therefore, virtually in the position of having to choose between, on the one hand, breaking off the negotiations altogether, or, on the other hand, accepting the American nominations, and appointing as their colleagues British Representatives appropriate to the altered circumstances of the case.

The British Government would prefer the tribunal to proceed. It therefore hoped that the Canadian Government would consider the names of British appointments.[27]

THE FOREIGN OFFICE FAIT ACCOMPLI

In the uncertainty of the previous two weeks the Foreign Office had kept its head best. On March 3, nearly three weeks after Senate approval of the treaty, it ordered Ambassador Herbert to exchange ratifications, that is, it ordered completion of the formalities of ratification without Canada's official consent. Secretary Hay had pressed for exchange of ratifications as early as February 14. Two weeks later, on February 28, Minto privately advised the Colonial Office, for the information of Lansdowne, that the Canadian Government would protestingly agree to the President's appointments,[28] and hence to the treaty. But the Canadian Government had not done so officially when it was confronted with the Foreign Office fait accompli — the exchange of ratifications.

Minto reported Laurier as "extremely annoyed" at this official ratification of the treaty, that he regarded this action as a " 'slap in the face for Canada,' " and that the country was "treated with discourtesy." However angry the Canadian Government was in private — there was a strong feeling to withdraw — on March 6 it made only a gesture of protest. It complained that *if* the matter was still open it would "hesitate to advise any further participation in proceedings" where there had been "so serious a departure from good faith." After ratification it was however "presumed that this fact precluded further discussion," a presumption which constitutionally was not true. This alleged constitutional inhibition masked the *political* reality that if Canada had dared to break off Roosevelt would have summoned Congress and got authority to draw the line. Nevertheless, Canada's dispatch continued, it reserved the right to submit the "whole correspondence" to the public with emphasis on "the manner in which the consent of Canada was obtained."[29] Canada exploited this grievance with singular effectiveness.

The Colonial Office supported Canada's protest. A. B. Keith protested against the Foreign Office's "blunder in tactics." Anderson emphasized that the "tone" of the Canadian telegram indicated that Canada was "washing its hands of responsibility in the matter, and will plead coercion in their Parlt. The result will be most deplorable, and it will cause more mischief in Canada than anything that has happened for years." The

Colonial Office therefore suggested to the Foreign Office that "as far as possible . . . the selection of Br. members" be in the hands of the Canadian Government.[30] Lansdowne concurred. It also requested that the Foreign Office write a reply to the Canadian cable of March 6. But the Colonial Office was only authorized to send a secret one to Lord Minto, the sense of which he might communicate to his ministers. On March 10 under Colonial Office signature the British Government denied it had treated the "Canadian interests with discourtesy." It seemed "of the utmost importance that the Convention should be concluded" and it believed that "the Canadian Government shared this view." The treaty had therefore been ratified.[31] We can only surmise the Foreign Office refusal to authorize an official reply: Canada might still break off.

There the matter might have temporarily rested had Laurier not demanded the right to publish all recent telegrams in a House of Commons debate. The Conservative leader, Robert L. Borden (later Sir Robert L.) blamed the government for lost opportunities. John Charlton tried to confront Canadians with the strategic facts of Canada's life: the overwhelming power of the United States and worldwide interests of Britain necessitating "good relations with the United States." A nation of five million could not dictate to one of eighty million. Henri Bourassa said the same except that he emphasized Britain's weakness rather than United States strength. Finally Laurier defended the treaty not as "arbitration" but as "judicial interpretation," though he later referred to it loosely as "arbitration." He also commented on the partiality of the United States appointments, concerning which Canada had made representations to Britain.[32]

On March 19 the Colonial Office received Canada's list of telegrams. A. B. Keith minuted: "If published they will rather tend to show that Canada was fooled into accepting the treaty by thinking U.S. judges would be appointed and that the treaty was inconsiderately ratified." In particular the list contained no official answer to Canada's March 6 telegram complaining of "so serious a departure from good faith." The Colonial Office had not replied because the telegram was "unanswerable."[33]

Anderson therefore summarized the whole affair for Chamberlain, who had recently returned from South Africa. The Colonial Office had forwarded the Canadian cables of complaint and its concurrence in the complaints to the Foreign Office. Under its own signature the Colonial Office had returned to Canada the Foreign Office reply of February 25. Colonial Office concurrence and the Foreign Office reply left no doubt that "it was still open to us to break off." While waiting for the formal Senate announcement of approval of the Hay-Herbert Treaty, the Colonial Office could not imagine that the Foreign Office had already obtained and sent ratification to Washington "for exchange, without warning the ambassador that he was not to do so until he received orders." This was how it appeared to the Colonial Office; in fact, the Foreign Office had ordered Herbert to "effect the exchange."[34] There was, however, no answer to the Canadian complaint of exchange of ratifications before receipt of Canada's reply. Chamberlain reacted in apparent support of his staff: "Inform F O by letter that I consider it very important to send specific answer to Canadian telegram which indicates intention on their part to lay whole blame on H.M.G. . . . . Draft for my approval."[35]

The gentlemanly contempt of the Foreign Office reply was ill concealed. It elaborately summarized the Colonial Office argument, reminded it of its March 10 letter, which it quoted *verbatim*. It cavalierly rejected the Colonial Office request for a letter in answer by explaining that it "would not have occured to His Lordship that any further answer was required." The letter then disclosed that "the ratification by the King took place on 17th February, and was announced upon the same day" in the King's speech opening Parliament, before the British Government had learned of the Canadian Government's attitude to the American appointments.[36]

Colonial Office officials were even angrier at this "most unsatisfactory" reply. A. B. Keith complained that "to put the onus" of ratification on the King was "utterly unconstitutional." Anderson expostulated that if Britain could not withdraw after February 17 why did the Foreign Office request the Colonial Office to write Canada opening that possibility? Furthermore the statement that Canada shared Britain's views was founded on Minto's telegram containing Laurier's views, and this telegram being "secret and personal" could not be published.[37] The problem was back on the Colonial Office doorstep. The Colonial Office therefore sent a telegram on April 2, 1903, containing the substance of the secret telegram to Lord Minto on March 10. In it Chamberlain re-emphasized the importance of the ratification of the treaty and the understanding that the British Government "had gathered from previous correspondence that while Ministers entertained strong objections to United States nominations they were not prepared to urge breaking off negotiations on that ground."[38]

The Colonial and the Foreign Offices were divided on the policy towards Canada, a division Canadian officials may have sensed. As early as July 20, 1901, Anderson objected to an even-numbered tribunal of six "and if a majority were secured by an *English* arbitrator going over to the Americans, the consequences would be most disastrous from a political point of view."[39] The supreme interest of the Colonial Office was harmonious relations between Britain and her colonies. The appointment of commissioners by Canada or withdrawal from the treaty would make Canada assume responsibilities of nationhood and take the burden of responsibility for a Canadian matter off Britain's back, and thereby preserve amicable Anglo-Canadian relations. The supreme interest of the Foreign Office was the maintenance of harmonious relations with foreign powers. And the power which in wartime could do Britain the most good was the United States; and two world wars validated that judgment. Hence the Foreign Office sacrificed Britain's colonial relationship to Canada for her international relationship with the United States.

There is no doubt that the Foreign Office argued speciously and acted in a Machiavellian manner. But given Britain's precarious international situation, Canada's sullen obstinacy and support by the Colonial Office, and the United States' determination to effect a settlement, what else could the Foreign Office have done? It could not be sure that Canada would not break off in anger. On February 17, evidently as a precaution against that possibility, it took unconstitutional advantage of King Edward VII's insistence on ratifying the treaty by letting him bear the responsibility rather than the Foreign Office, and ratification was announced in the King's speech. Although the February 25 cable indicated that the Foreign Office wanted Canada's support it would not wait for Canada's notorious delays. Having learned of Canada's probable approval and observed that Canada had not yet broken off, it was prepared to risk Canada's anger rather than Roosevelt's breaking off, for he also had been reluctant to accept the treaty.[40]

And so a student need not sob with Professor C. S. Campbell, Jr.: "Poor Canada! Step by step she had been beaten down."[41] Chamberlain's forthright reply to the complaint of the Canadian Minister of Finance, W. S. Fielding, that Canada had been "shamefully treated" is a sufficient answer.

> . . . I gathered from Sir Wilfrid Laurier when he was here that it was a primary interest with Canada to get this matter settled even if you did not secure the recognition of your full conditions.

Though rightly objecting to the United States nominations

> you were not prepared to break off of that account. . . . If this is the correct view of your position I do not exactly see where our fault lies. The exchange of ratifications was a purely formal matter, although, if the Canadian Government had really been prepared to throw everything once more into the crucible, I suppose it might have been possible to take the unusual course of refusing to ratify. There is no doubt what the result would have been. The United States would have taken the law into their own hands, and Canada as well as we would have found ourselves face to face with a most critical situation which I believe it was the intention and the interest of the Canadian Government to avoid. . . . Do you wish the so-called arbitration to fail? . . . In fact, is a settlement of the first importance, or is it better to give up all hope of a settlement rather than accept a decision which would be more or less unpalatable to the Canadian people?[42]

Confronted with the stark alternative of humiliation or catastrophe, which Canadians forebodingly sensed rather than spelled out, Canadians understandably seized the opportunity of blaming Britain for actions of questionable constitutionality, which Britain's and Canada's necessity had dictated. Canada was also to discover that this was the first instalment of its humiliation.

Chapter VI

Canada Big-Sticked:
II The Alaska Boundary Tribunal
1903

In the twenty years since Canadians had been re-asserting the presumed treaty line, Canadian leaders had tended to be over-concerned with internal political problems and to disregard external political reality. By trusting in Britain's power or rather the power of Imperial unity, which they would not recognize as declining, they tended to be blind to the mounting power of the United States. Now Canadians were paying the price in the making and the implementing of the Hay-Herbert Treaty in the United States insistence on the letter of the treaty during the preparation of Canadian arguments, and in the contemptuous nature of the tribunal's decision.[1]

PERSONNEL AND PREPARATION OF ARGUMENTS

Yet Laurier's initial preparations seemed wise and cautious. He obtained Britain's consent for the selection of the Lord Chief Justice — Lord Alverstone — as senior British Commissioner on the tribunal. The Canadian Commissioners were Sir Louis Jetté, Lieutenant-Governor of Quebec and former member of its Supreme Court, and Justice George Armour of the Supreme Court of Canada, and on the latter's death, Allen B. Aylesworth, a distinguished Toronto lawyer. In contrast to the American political appointments, British appointments were judicial. Canada also selected the British Agent, Clifford Sifton, who was charged with the diplomacy, the administrative oversight, and the preparation of the British case. It also selected the counsel: Christopher Robinson, a distinguished Toronto lawyer, and Edward Blake, former Minister of Justice and leader of the Liberal party. Having once agreed to these appointments Britain was almost guiltily lavish in assisting Canada in the preparation and presentation of the arguments. It offered as one of the counsel the services of the Attorney-General — Sir Robert (later Lord) Finlay. When Edward Blake's overwork resulted in a nervous breakdown Canada also obtained the services of the Solicitor-General, Sir Edward Carson. Canada also employed the Solicitor for the Treasury, Sidney (afterwards Sir Sidney) A. T. Rowlatt, who apparently did the initial drafting of the arguments and who, together with F. C. Wade, a Manitoba lawyer who had been legal adviser of the Yukon Council (1897-1901), did most of the preparation. Of the other Canadians, mention need only be made here of Joseph Pope, the best informed Canadian and virtual secretary of the British delegation (later an assistant secretary of the tribunal itself) and W. F. King, Surveyor-General of Canada. Sir John Anderson, one of the best informed on the question in Britain, made himself freely available. British authorities also provided the delegation with experts in international law, geography, hydrography, and translation. Finally Britain agreed to share joint costs equally with Canada.

This was a competent, industrious, and experienced delegation. Alverstone, Finlay, Rowlatt, Anderson, Robinson, and Pope had all been present in some official capacity at the Bering Sea Arbitration Tribunal (1892-93). The first three also served at the Venezuela Boundary Arbitration (1899). The nationality of the personnel and the amount of expert assistance demonstrate, however, that the preparation and presentation were more British than Canadian. These facts, together with Sifton's undue deference to Anderson's views, suggest the same tactics as Canada used at the Joint High Commission: put as much onus on Britain as possible. Laurier indeed called the British section of the tribunal the "Court of Imperial Jurists."[2]

From the outset pessimism pervaded the Canadian camp. Canadians believed that the best they could expect was a draw, and hopefully a subsequent diplomatic settlement, a possibility that they did not know President Roosevelt had ruled out.

Initially, too, Sifton was very bitter at Britain's conduct in the Hay-Herbert Treaty. Writing to J. W. Dafoe, editor of the *Manitoba Free Press,* he complained of the "cold-blooded" giving away of Canada's interests without having "a fight for it." He had observed British diplomacy yielding to American demands in Canadian affairs.[3] He seemed unaware that Britain had had to yield and forgotten the Venezuela Incident and its implications.

To make "a fight for it" was exactly what Sifton intended to do. Choate noted that the Canadians were "working like beavers,"[4] had the run of government departments, the Public Record Office, the British Museum, and the Hudson's Bay Company. Indeed the work of the British delegation seems almost frenzied in its ramifications. Considerable preparation and thought had been given to the case before leaving Canada, but not much to subsequent arguments, that is, to foreseeing American arguments and the strategy of combatting them. A comparison of the amount of documentation attached to the British

Sir Clifford Sifton
during the Alaska boundary
arbitration in London.

Case and its Counter-Case, 350 to 80 pages respectively, suggests this conclusion.

By contrast the American delegation never forgot strategy, knew where it was going, and often treated Canadians contemptuously, principally by a ruthless and narrow adherence to the letter of the treaty. It exploited every avenue of influence. Its agent was John W. Foster, experienced as agent in the Bering Sea Arbitration and in his third international conference opposite Canadians. He was an expert on the Alaska boundary question and an adviser thereon to the State Department. In the preparation of the American arguments for the tribunal he received invaluable advice from Ambassador Joseph Choate, one of America's leading lawyers. Choate declined appointment as America's senior counsel before the boundary tribunal because of his confidential relations with British officials. Nevertheless Choate, together with John Hay and Henry White, had all been intimately connected with the diplomacy of the Alaska boundary question for five years. Behind these four Americans loomed a President itching for action. On the British side, except perhaps for Sifton, there was no expert of such comparable political and public stature. Joseph Pope and Sir John Anderson were civil servants.

SIFTON'S POLITICAL BLUNDERS

In spite of the beaver-like industry of the British delegation it was pressed for time, but whenever it requested or demanded an extension of time, which was permitted under the treaty, the United States was adamant in opposition. To the first suggestion in March, Herbert warned that Washington might be suggested as the tribunal meeting place — and Canada withdrew the request. In April Alverstone requested postponement of the delivery of the oral argument. Hay was absolutely opposed: a "fait accompli" would prevent discussion in Congress.[5]

The third request — or rather demand — was much more serious. The American Case — 110 pages long with 550 pages of documentation — arrived in Britain on May 11; and this left fifty-one days for preparation of the British Counter-Case. Anderson complained of the American Case to Sifton and observed that several translations of Russian documents read like "clotted nonsense." Could not Foster be called upon at once for permission "to let us inspect the originals and if possible have them photographed? He is so full of tricks I wd not trust him with a three-penny bit." Sifton consented, and oddly in view of the pressure of time, on May 14, 1903, *wrote* the request to Foster in Washington instead of *cabling* him.[6] Instead of requesting a few documents Ambassador Herbert was instructed both to demand the right to photograph 200 pages of documents and to request an extension of time.

These demands were objectionable on four grounds. In the first place Hay sardonically suggested in the bitter correspondence between the American and British Governments that the British side could not "allege" having "been taken by surprise by the Case of the United States." Correspondence since 1898 gave "ample time" to "the Canadian authorities to prepare their case."[7] Why, indeed, had not Canadians made a careful examination of their case? One reason was Canada's lack of a department of external affairs continuously studying all the ramifications of the question. Another was Laurier's periodic and moody pessimism, which probably concealed from himself his own basic disbelief in the Canadian case, and prevented his officially authorizing Joseph Pope to keep the problem under continuous scrutiny.

Secondly, even as an aid to argument, Joseph Pope's Washington investigation and photography of many of the 200 pages of American documents was futile. Pope reported that between his own analysis and the American version 99% of the documents examined did not differ materially! Furthermore as early as June 9, S. A. T. Rowlatt had informed Sifton that after a second perusal of the American documents the facts of the case could be taken "as practically ascertained"!! Even so on August 10 the British delegation requested similar examination and photographing privileges of the Counter-Case documents. But as the documents were being shipped to London Foster informed Sifton they could be examined there, and on August 31 Sifton was so informed. In the "Final Report of the Agent of the United States" Foster sardonically reported to Hay that "no inspection took place of the documents in the counter case, and no reference was ever made to the inspection had in Washington, either in the British printed argument or in the proceedings before the Tribunal"!!![8] No wonder American leaders made frequent reference to the "stupid" policies of the Canadians.

Thirdly if the requests were practically stupid they were even more politically stupid. Hay objected to the "sweeping" request and complained that "in no other instance can it be recalled that such a complete impeachment of the American case has ever been made."[9] A request to see about two-thirds of the American documentary evidence (apart from previously published evidence) was bound to make the United States angry. Why did the normally politically astute Sifton ignore the political implications of this request? When he saw how British officials put themselves out to help Canada in preparing the Alaska boundary case his attitude towards Britain appears to have softened. Increasingly Sifton deferred to Anderson's judgment, and during Sifton's absence in Canada from June 17 to September 1 Anderson was virtually British agent. That is, Canada was almost reverting to a colonial relationship with Britain, and Britain's support of Canada seemed to be being tested.

The British delegation also demanded an extension of time in order that the fruits of Pope's investigation be used in the British Counter-Case. Hay refused and promised the privilege of examination on condition that the British Counter-Case arrived on time — July 3. After advice from the Colonial Office, the Foreign Office replied that to couple production of documents with extension of time amounted to a "refusal . . . without an extension of time." Hay argued legalistically and even speciously against granting an extension; for example, under Article II a document need not be produced for seventy days. Whereupon Britain threatened to break off. There can be little doubt that this threat was to impress the Canadians, for Hay's casual reference to the failure of "Canadian authorities to prepare their case" suggests his awareness that Britain was the advocate and Canada the principal. In the end the British authorities submitted the Counter-Case on time with only about eighty pages of documentation.[10]

ROOSEVELT'S UGLY PRESSURE FOR A FAVOURABLE DECISION

The fourth and most serious consequence of the Canadian demands was the apparent effect on President Roosevelt. In late March Roosevelt had read a summary newspaper account of Laurier's parliamentary speech on the Hay-Herbert Treaty and the American appointments. He was angry, and erroneously interpreted Laurier's observations as meaning that Canadian appointees to the tribunal were "to uphold" Canada's claims "as advocates rather than . . . as judges." As he considered "these claims as untenable," he set forth his own views in his instructions of March 17, 1903, to the American Commissioners. Although they were to judge the questions impartially, the claim to ports on the Lynn Canal could not "be properly considered open to discussion." By the Treaty of 1825 the lisière was intended to cut England off from the sea. Although he admitted there was room for dispute as to its width, on the principle of a continuous strip "there will of course be no compromise."[11]

Two months apparently elapsed before the Alaskan boundary question next figured prominently in Roosevelt's considerations. During Ambassador Choate's visit to the United States for his son's wedding in June he was instructed to go to Washington for discussion of boundary matters. The Ambassador also participated in an important conference on the White House porch together with the Secretaries of State, War, and the President. There Choate, Hay, and Root apparently agreed with Roosevelt's plan to dispatch troops if the tribunal failed to reach a majority decision. Senators Lodge and Turner, and apparently Foster, were informed of this contingency plan. The statement issued on November, 1903, intended for publication to justify seizure of Panama if the Panama Revolution had not taken place, demonstrates that Roosevelt's intention regarding Alaska was then not a bluff.[12] The United States had bullied Britain into submission in the Venezuela Incident of 1895-96, and was in a much stronger position to do so in 1903.

What prompted the White House conference at that time? Choate's presence provided the opportunity, but recent Canadian demands probably produced the occasion. Two weeks later Roosevelt denounced the British demand for delay. In a letter of June 23, 1903, to Roosevelt, Senator Lodge had objected to that demand because of the need to return to the United States in time for the next session of Congress. He therefore suggested postponement of the tribunal meetings until the summer of 1904; this "would bring them to time. If we take a stiff tone I am sure it would." In his next letter of June 27, 1903, Lodge complained that the "British are trying to crowd us." Lodge's letters set off a jingoistic mood that apparently possessed Roosevelt until the boundary was settled. In reply on June 29, 1903, Roosevelt reacted even more emotionally than Lodge by expressing himself as against postponement and threatening Britain with unilateral United States action if Britain failed to comply with the treaty.[13]

It took all Hay's powers to dissuade Roosevelt from contemplating this jingo use of power. The United States, Hay argued on July 2, was "doing exactly what you suggest — resisting . . . every attempt at delay." They (the Canadians) were not "acting in bad faith" but using "every possible pretext" for more time "to patch up their deplorably weak case." Choate's latest telegram indicated that the British delegation would submit their Counter-Case on July 3:

> Foster's worst enemy would never accuse him of any tendency to mercy or tenderness to an opponent. The treaty *does* allow for more time in special exigencies — but we are fighting to show they have no right to it now. You remember we crowded them out of two months they wanted, in the negotiation of the treaty . . . .
>
> I do not think any threats at this time advisable or needful.
>
> We shall be as hard on them as is decent — perhaps rather more so.[14]

This letter together with letters from White and Choate brought Roosevelt back to a modicum of sense.

On receipt of Lodge's telegram suggesting that Roosevelt should break off, Roosevelt sharply opposed Lodge's suggestion, and gave him not an "'official and authoritative'" instruction but a private letter to be shown to British leaders. In it the President stressed the need to report a decision to Congress, emphasizing that he had gone "very far . . . to come to a friendly understanding with England", and twice repeated that this was to be the "last chance."[15] This was the first of a series of Rooseveltian threats to intimidate British authorities.

A few days later, on July 25, Roosevelt wrote his well-known letter to Supreme Court Justice Oliver Wendell Holmes, which he too was authorized to show to British leaders. Holmes had reported to Roosevelt that Chamberlain found it hard to understand how Roosevelt could send commissioners to England with their minds already made up, like Senator Lodge. Roosevelt's reply, though like the letter to Lodge, stated the alternative more bluntly:

> But if there is a disagreement I wish it to be distinctly understood . . . that in my message to Congress I shall take a position . . . to give me authority to run the line as we claim it, . . . without any further regard to the attitude of England and Canada . . . .[16]

Lodge showed his letter to Balfour, Chamberlain, Harcourt (Sir William V., former Liberal Party leader), and Alverstone. He also wrote to Lansdowne who was in Ireland. It was not the English, he wrote to his daughter, who were making trouble, but the Canadians. "That collection of bumptious provincials bullies" the English, who were silenced by them. Only by accepting could the "stupid" Canadians escape "creditably." If they did not Roosevelt would say the territory was now American. In response to this pressure, Balfour wrote to Alverstone urging conciliation, and Lansdowne spoke to him emphasizing the need for a settlement which Alverstone promised he would do his best to bring about.[17]

In the meantime Canada's fourth demand for delay — this time in the presentation of the oral argument — infuriated Roosevelt and other American leaders. In part this demand was a result of misunderstanding. The Hay-Herbert Treaty provided for the submission of the written argument on September 3, the same date as the initial meeting of the tribunal, which itself would determine the date of the oral argument. As the American Case and the Counter-Case after delivery in Washington arrived in London on May 11 and about July 11 respectively, it was natural to suppose that the American written argument would arrive about September 11, but American dispatches were imprecise on this point. Sifton therefore asked for the oral argument to begin on October 15. Choate complained to Hay bitterly of Sifton's "audacious proposition . . . I can't stand their dawdling" and he was "very glad" to have stirred them up. A bitter exchange of correspondence took place until the British delegation comprehended that the United States written argument was being delivered in London on September 3. The tribunal did meet on that day but adjourned until September 15, when the oral argument began. Lord Alverstone exonerated Sifton, explaining that the demand for delay came from the Attorney-General [Finlay]. But American leaders already knew that Alverstone himself had once requested delay because it interfered with his shooting.[18]

English officials protested vainly against the crudity of American pressure. Lord Lansdowne thought the United States much too " 'hard on' " Canadians, and F. H. Villiers of the Foreign Office protested "against our crowding them so."[19]

ALVERSTONE'S HEROIC RESISTANCE TO AMERICAN PRESSURE

Lord Alverstone has gone down in Canadian history as one of Canada's great traitors. Alverstone was not a traitor to Canada, but a Victorian of considerable character. His conduct during the meetings of the Alaska Boundary Tribunal shows him to have been a tragic and unfairly maligned figure. He had to bear alone the onus of an unpopular decision that the British Government had dumped on him. The inner story of the meetings and of Alverstone's decision may never be fully known because our present information comes from triumphant American sources and resentful Canadian ones. British sources, for several reasons, are noticeably deficient. Britain's conduct during the making of the Hay-Herbert Treaty and subsequent pressure on Lord Alverstone could not be defended openly. Secondly, in preserving the unofficial Anglo-American entente, British leaders had learned to be very wary of expressing public or private opinions on the United States or on Anglo-American relations. Finally in September and October, 1903, Britain was in a dangerous international situation with Japan, Russia, France, and Germany.[20] Thus it was essential for Britain to maintain friendship with the United States.

Meanwhile Roosevelt's war of nerves against Canada continued in London. Canadians later said it was an open secret in London that Canada was going to lose, and the wife of an

Canadian Annual Review, 1902

The Right Hon. Lord Alverstone, G.C.M.G., LL.D., Lord Chief Justice of England and President of the Alaska Boundary Tribunal.

American Commissioner said so in front of Mrs. Aylesworth.[21] Canadians tried to combat this propaganda by inspiring newspaper articles demanding that Britain support Canada. Roosevelt was so furious at Canadian pressure that Hay again had to restrain him in a letter of September 25 from exercising "cowboy diplomacy":

> I had seen this article already and had written to Harry White — so that it might indiscreetly percolate through to Balfour — that it would be a deplorable thing if this Canadian bulldozing succeeded; that I knew, both from Pauncefote and Laurier, that they had no belief in their case; that you were brought to consent to this Tribunal purely through your desire for good relations & the settlement of a vexed question honorably to England; that if the Tribunal failed to agree, it would end the matter; that we should hold the property that belongs to us, of our right to which we have never had the shadow of a doubt; that neither you, nor any American President would ever make another attempt to facilitate the escape of Canada from an absolutely untenable position.
>
> Of course the matter is now *sub judice*. You can say nothing about it. . . . But I am sure Harry White will leave no doubt of the true state of the case in the mind of the Prime Minister.

White reported his visit to Balfour's home in Scotland with the warning that the United States wanted a decision and his subsequent meeting with Balfour's secretary J. S. Sandars, who, he said, twice interviewed Lord Alverstone.[22] At the sessions of the tribunal, of which Alverstone had been elected president, Lodge asserted to Roosevelt that he watched Alverstone to see what British arguments appealed to him, and later tried to counter them. All this pressure, bluster, and affirmation of a prospective American victory suggest considerable doubt in the minds of Americans that the United States could win easily and unmistakably.

Accordingly, Lord Alverstone became the centre of rival American and Canadian pressures, while Alverstone tried to maintain a judicial stance. In the early sessions Canadians became angry because he seemed not a British leader but an umpire between Canada and the United States. But the implied analogy between the Joint High Commission of 1898-99 and the Alaska Boundary Tribunal was false; the former was frankly political and the latter in form judicial, though the political use of the tribunal by the United States forced Canada into doing the same. In fact, however, Alverstone put up an heroic battle against the Americans for justified Canadian claims. His tactics appeared to have been to show friendliness to Americans and keep his distance from Canadians in order to make Americans think he was leaning towards their position. But this tactic often deceived Canadians into believing that he was yielding to Americans and even using Canadian confidences for the defeat of Canadians.

Thus Alverstone invited Joseph Pope to his estate for a weekend to sound him on official Canadian hopes. He had come to know Pope at the Bering Sea Arbitration in the 1890s. Would Canada, Alverstone inquired on September 13, 1903, be satisfied with the Portland Canal area and a "good" mountain line? Speaking personally, Pope said that Canada would prefer deadlock to exclusion from ports on the lisière. To Alverstone's objection that this was unreasonable Pope replied that the "Government had to consider their political position as well as the intrinsic merits of the dispute." A few days later Pope reported official Canadian hopes to Alverstone: Canada would be satisfied with Portland Canal and a "good" mountain line, for it could be maintained that Canada had "won two contentions out of three." Pope received the impression from Alverstone that "I can't get you the inlets — but trust me for the rest!"[23]

That this was the correct impression is proved by Anderson's report of a conversation with Alverstone. Three days after the oral argument began (September 18, 1903) Sifton complained to Anderson that he had received the impression that Alverstone had yielded on the inlets and that this concession would enable the Americans to hold out for the mountain range and Portland Canal. He therefore asked him to request the British Government to instruct Alverstone to let the tribunal come to a deadlock or postpone its sessions until after the United States election of 1904. Anderson warned Sifton that it was "unheard of" for the government to dictate a judge's course of action, and that Alverstone might resign, the circumstances would leak out, and the Canadian position be "irretrievably ruined." Sifton replied that Canada would be in no worse state. Anderson therefore asked Sifton to think it over for a day.

When Anderson told Alverstone of Sifton's fears, Alverstone denied that he had made up his mind. Did Sifton really believe, Alverstone inquired, that Canada would get the inlets as the "impracticable" Aylesworth and Jetté did? Anderson said no, but Sifton was anxious for the Portland Canal boundary and "the Canadian line up to the Lynn Canal." Alverstone answered " 'I can do much better for him than that.' " When Anderson next saw Sifton, Sifton reported Aylesworth and Jetté as more optimistic, and therefore did not want the British Government approached.[24]

On October 7, the day before the end of the oral argument, however, Sifton cabled Laurier the fears of Aylesworth and Jetté: that Alverstone intended "to join Americans" and they were "considering withdrawing from Commission." Laurier cabled that the Commissioners should fight on:

> Our Commissioners must not withdraw. If they cannot get our full rights let them put up a bitter fight for our contention on Portland Canal, which is beyond doubt: that point must be decided in Canada's favour. Shame Chief Justice and carry that point. If we are thrown over by Chief Justice, he will give the last blow to British diplomacy in Canada. He should be plainly told this by our Commissioners.[25]

These fears were not yet well founded. When the Commissioners reconvened on October 12 to reach their final decisions Alverstone handed the Canadian Commissioners a printed statement declaring that the four islands in the Portland Inlet were Canadian. His doing so suggests the tremendous American pressure upon him. Alverstone had decided to cast his vote for the American possession of the inlets and for the Canadian possession of the four islands and a mountain line close to the sea. Lodge was opposed to what he called Alverstone's "doctrine of selected summits," a phrase denying the existence of a coast range. Indeed as late as October 14 Lodge reported Alverstone as arguing for this "with great force & some heat."[26]

Up to October 14 the American war of nerves and direct pressure on Alverstone had failed. Perhaps British officials were bored by Roosevelt's interminable letters and warnings sent through Lodge, Holmes, Hay, and White. Lodge must have been nursing Roosevelt's "man-on-horseback" tendencies when he wrote to Roosevelt that the arguments made "no earthly difference" to the tribunal decisions, which depended on the "Commissioners" not on "arguments."[27] This was not yet true, but it required a direct and carefully planned official intervention of Ambassador Choate to compel the British Prime Minister and/or the Foreign Secretary to make it true.

As the official representative of the United States Government, Choate on October 15 now saw Lansdowne alone and enjoined him not to set the interview on paper. After repeating the usual Rooseveltian threats about there never being another agreement and the summoning of Congress to authorize the drawing of the boundary line, Choate called upon the British Government to support Alverstone, who was "hard beset by the Canadians." This apparently was the only way Americans could explain Alverstone's obstinacy. According to Choate's report, Lansdowne asked Choate what he would suggest. Choate suggested that the four Commissioners should draw the line, or if necessary, Choate and Lansdowne might agree on a suitable line and inform the Commissioners of their thinking. Choate left the interview confident that Alverstone would be instructed, but he did not report the interview to Hay until October 20, the day of decision.[28]

SITKLAN AND KANNAGHUNUT

His rear protected, Choate now sent to Hay on behalf of the American Commissioners an important cable outlining the situation and suggesting a "compromise." The evidence, the cable explained, permitted a line north of Pearse and Wales Islands, implying that it went south of Sitklan and Kannaghunut, though the two latter islands were not named. As for the fifth question Alverstone "stands stiffly" for mountains nearest the shore "giving us a strip only a few miles wide along the shore." If the United States held out for a ten-league strip it might lead to disagreement on all questions. Furthermore since the survey treaty of 1892 left the centre of the ten-league strip incomplete over most of its length there was no way to prove that any line in that area was not the true line. Choate therefore proposed that experts provided for under Article I of the Hay-Herbert Treaty complete the survey, which would be rendered after November 1904. Since the English member insisted on "the principle of running line along summits of mountains nearest the sea," even if an acceptable compromise could be agreed upon, additional surveys were necessary for a "tenable theory" to uphold the line. "Would an adjournment . . . be preferable," it concluded.

Hay's reply reached London on October 17, 1903. If question 5 were favourable to the American contention, that is, Canada was cut off from the inlets, the President would not object to adjournment for those purposes. A "most confidential" and important postscript, however, authorized the line to be run along the north channel of Portland Canal. Suggestions for adjournment without fundamental decisions being made were certainly not to be taken seriously, since earlier reasons against adjournment still obtained.[29] Moreover since mid-September a new factor had entered the situation making a decision by the tribunal essential — the prospect of a Panama revolution. For the United States to have been divided from Britain over an unsettled Alaska boundary might have produced serious diplomatic embarrassment.

As Choate's telegram to Hay indicated, Alverstone was more resistant to American arguments and pressures than anticipated. This meant that when Alverstone was forced to yield the decision would be a political compromise, and no "tenable theory" would justify a compromise, which Senator Turner declared essential. The American solution was to conceal the absence of a tenable theory by enraging naive Canadians into believing that they had abjectly lost in the Alaska Boundary Tribunal. On September 15 Roosevelt replied to a letter from Hay that the "little islands," probably Sitklan and Kannaghunut, could be used as a "make-weight" if necessary. On the next day in London while Sir Robert Finlay in the oral argument was tracing the movements of Captain Vancouver down the Portland Canal or the "North Channel," as the Americans called it, north of Wales and Pearse Islands, Turner intervened to suggest that Vancouver had emerged at the entrance of two channels: the one to the west, north of Sitklan and Kannaghunut Islands and the other between Sitklan and Wales Islands. Was it not possible, Turner inquired, that the channel between Wales and Sitklan Islands was part of Portland Canal? This second possibility had hitherto never appeared in any of the literature on the subject. In the ensuing discussion which several times bobbed up in the next few minutes Turner admitted that Vancouver had not passed down that channel but had sailed west past its entrance. Although Finlay demonstrated that the passage westerly was what Vancouver understood as Portland Canal, Turner had raised the possibility of Portland Canal passing between Wales and Sitklan islands.[30]

A month later on October 17 after the Lord Chief Justice had been instructed by the Prime Minister and/or the Foreign Secretary to yield to American demands, the line between Wales and Sitklan Islands was made the boundary. The Aylesworth account of the meeting on that day, four years after the event, indicates that Alverstone and the three Americans had made arrangements beforehand. Alverstone began the meeting by asking each Commissioner his opinion on the disposition of the four islands. Root began and spoke for "about an hour" claiming all the islands for the United States; Jetté, unprepared, made a few remarks; Lodge "or" Turner agreed with Root; Aylesworth said he agreed with Alverstone's printed memorandum of October 12 that the four islands belonged to Canada. Alverstone apparently then put the question, did Portland Channel go north or south of Pearse and Wales Islands? The Canadians were astonished when the three Americans voted that it went north, that is, that these two islands belonged to Canada. Then Alverstone asked, does Portland Channel go north or south of Sitklan and Kannaghunut Islands? The Canadians' astonishment turned to dismay when they saw Alverstone vote with the three Americans that the line went south, that is, that the two islands belonged to the United States. Alverstone explained that it "pained him to have to decide against his own country . . . otherwise there would be no agreement. . . ." Thereupon Aylesworth "denounced him vigorously."[31] This division of the islands was unwarranted in precedent or argument, though its possibility had been hinted at during the oral argument.

Since Alverstone had committed himself only five days earlier to Canada's ownership of the four islands he had to justify their division. He now argued that when Vancouver sailed down the Portland Canal past Pearse and Wales Islands "he may have intended" the passage between Wales and Sitklan Islands as the continuance of Portland Canal. This argument was not only "specious" but careless, for Alverstone's written judgment on this part of the decision was a careless redrafting of his judgment of October 12. Furthermore while the body of the Alverstone's argument gave Canada two islands, the conclusion only on the copy Sifton received gave Canada four islands, which suggests Alverstone had a guilty conscience. Embarrassed, the Foreign Office a week later sent Sifton a corrected copy initialed by Alverstone.[32]

John S. Ewart in his famous essay on "The Alaska Boundary" (1908), written in bitter animus, which Aylesworth and Jetté "read and corrected" before publication, compared the two Alverstone versions (October 12 and 20, 1903) and demonstrated how small were the changes in the second, except for one paragraph. Ewart attacked Alverstone's " 'treachery' " and was incensed at his carelessness, of which he had already seen evidence in 1892 in the appeal of the Manitoba School Case before the Judicial Committee of the Privy Council.[33] In view of Alverstone's earlier resistance to American pressure, may not his carelessness at this point have been due not only to a guilty conscience but also to unconscious sympathy for the brutal treatment of Canada and to self-disgust at his own humiliation, which few British Chief Justices must ever have been subjected to by a government of the day? On the other hand he could not resign for he would have been warned of Roosevelt's intentions had there been no agreement.

The mountain line on the strip was also a compromise, of course denying access to the inlets, except that a gap of 120 miles was left unmarked between the Stikine and Taku Rivers. The award explained the gap as follows: although the line marked on the map followed the mountains referred to as paralleling the coast, the incompleteness of the survey north of the Stikine prevented a similar type of demarcation in that region. In the popular understanding of the award this gap was generally overlooked. Unofficial maps tended to fill in the gap with the usual map line.

On the day of decision — October 17 — an enraged Sifton cabled Laurier the essential features of the decision: "Chief Justice has agreed with American Commissioners. Their decision" would give Canada Wales and Pearse islands and the United States Sitklan and Kannaghunut, "which command entrance to canal and destroy strategic value Wales and Pearce [sic]", a statement that Laurier almost certainly interpreted as asking approval of Sifton's subsequent mode of protest. This seems to have been the first reference at this time to the strategic value of the islands. "Remainder of line substantially contended for by Americans . . . I regard it as wholly indefensible. What is your view? Course of discussion between Commissioners has greatly exasperated our Commissioners who consider matter as pre-arranged."

Laurier replied in the same angry tone supplying further arguments for a Canadian protest:

> Ottawa, October 18th. Concession to Americans of Kanaghannut [sic] and Sitklan cannot be justified on any consideration of treaty. It is one of those concessions which have made British diplomacy odious to Canadian people, and it will have a most lamentable effect. Our Commissioners ought to protest in most vigorous terms.[34]

And so on October 20, 1903, exactly four years after the previous defeat in the *modus vivendi* of October 20, 1899, the award was officially signed without public ceremony. Lodge described "Canadians sullenly refusing to discuss anything & announcing that they would not sign any part of the award, which was silly but makes the extent of our victory very clear in America."[35] This was almost certainly the purpose of the division of the islands: to infuriate Canadians and create the illusion of an American boundary victory, which in turn would conceal the absence of a tenable theory.

It is surely now no longer necessary to raise the ludicrous question, was the decision judicial or political? Of course it

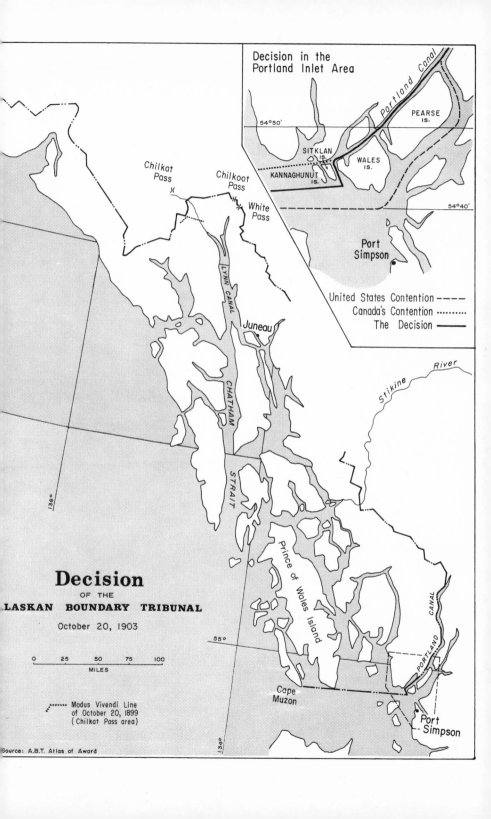

Decision in the
Portland Inlet Area

Portland Canal

PEARSE
IS.

54°50'

SITKLAN
IS.

WALES
IS.

KANNAGHUNUT
IS.

54°40'

Port
Simpson

United States Contention ----
Canada's Contention ....
The Decision ——

Chilkat
Pass

Chilkoot
Pass

White
Pass

LYNN CANAL

Juneau

CHATHAM STRAIT

Stikine River

138°

Prince of Wales Island

PORTLAND CANAL

Decision
OF THE
ALASKAN BOUNDARY TRIBUNAL

October 20, 1903

0	25	50	75	100

MILES

55°

Cape
Muzon

Port
Simpson

136°

.... Modus Vivendi Line
of October 20, 1899
(Chilkat Pass area)

Source: A.B.T. Atlas of Award

was political — on all sides. The United States was more successful because it was more powerful and had the better case. Actually except for the division of the four islands and the line extending twenty miles beyond the temporary boundary in the Chilkat Pass area, the boundary decision was a reasonable compromise. It was practically a re-assertion of the Russian map line which had remained unchallenged for nearly 60 years.

But the American political victory was no illusion: Canada suffered a humiliation of great magnitude. By depriving Canada of any tenable theory of justifying the boundary between the islands, the United States appeared to be able to dictate Canadian boundaries. This was a harsh truth no Canadian dared — or need — face. He could accuse Lord Alverstone of "treachery" for violating his judicial oath and for failure to support Canadian interests. Thus he could deny the aggressiveness of American policy and the stupidity of his own.

Canada Blames Britain

Hitherto historians of the Alaska award have described Canada's explosive resentment in indiscriminate generalization. They have noted Canada's demand for control of external relations and asserted that the settlement was in the best interests of Canada itself. Such interpretations take too much for granted: they ignore the pattern of protest and especially its potent anti-Americanism; they tend to slide over responsibility of each of the three countries; and they fail to analyze the long-run effects of the decision on Canadians in their relations with Americans.

On the day after the award (October 21, 1903) the Canadian Commissioners issued a protest, which Sifton and Aylesworth had spent the previous night in preparing, justifying their refusal to sign. It began by analyzing rival claims to the four disputed islands in Portland Inlet. Although the British Commissioner asserted in a memorandum that Canada's contention was "absolutely unanswerable," in the final award a majority of the Commissioners gave Canada two islands and the United States two. The latter two "command the entrance to Portland Channel, to Observatory Inlet and the ocean passage to Port Simpson" and destroyed "the strategic value to Canada of Wales and Pearse Islands." Nor had such a line ever before been advocated. As for the line north from Portland Canal, the tribunal found the Canadian contention regarding the existence of mountains correct but disregarded their existence by fixing the line "to give the United States . . . nearly all of the territory in dispute," and this formed a "complete land barrier." Thus the decision was not "judicial" but a sacrifice of the "interests" and "just rights of Canada."[1]

In similar, longer, and more legalistic vein both Jetté and

Aylesworth also made official protests which Sifton had insisted upon. Jetté's was somewhat milder than Aylesworth's, which *inter alia* referred to the loss of Sitklan and Kannaghunut as a "grotesque travesty of justice." Sifton in effect also made a public protest.[2]

Was it true that Sitklan and Kannaghunut, about fourteen miles from Port Simpson, were a strategic loss to Canada? For more than fifteen years Canadians had believed in the strategic value of Portland Inlet, as a Canadian gateway to the fabulous Orient and, during the railway mania of 1903, Port Simpson was regarded as the future terminus of three transcontinentals. Actually both Sitklan, four square miles in area with a maximum elevation of 350 feet, and Kannaghunut, less than three square miles with a maximum elevation of 150 feet, were strategically worthless. Artillery set up on peaks more than 1000 feet high on Wales Island and *on adjoining American peaks* all within a range of five miles could dominate Sitklan and Kannaghunut; and the United States Navy, already in virtual control of the northeast Pacific, would have made such artillery unnecessary.

CANADA'S RAGE AGAINST ALVERSTONE AND BRITAIN

When the news of the decision reached Canada headlines flared across the country's press: Canada had been "sacrificed," "robbed," "tricked."[3] S. E. Gourley, the Canadian Imperialist from Nova Scotia, cried out in Parliament as a man bitterly hurt and betrayed:

> we have been wronged out of this territory . . . absolutely wronged . . . I point to this government as the occasion of the enormous humiliation to which the people of Canada have been subjected. I confess that I have been humiliated past endurance for a week.[4]

The tribunal seemed a trick got up to gull innocent Canadians naively expecting American generosity. The ugly forebodings that the Hay-Herbert Treaty had conjured up had come only too true. Was this Canada's reward for assistance in the Boer War?

"Canada seems to have been butchered by Alverstone to make a United States holiday," vituperated the Ottawa *Journal* on October 23. Canadians complained that he betrayed Canadian interests and acted not "as a jurist but as a diplomat." Why could he not have stood by Canada as Lord Herschell had done five years earlier? The Hamilton *Herald* was revolted that

> Lord Alverstone weakly and shamefully yielded to the American commissioners, agreeing to cede to the United States important territory which he had asserted to be rightfully belonging to Canada. . . . But if he was capable of acting dishonorably in one detail he was capable of dishonorable conduct in another. . . . [He was] acting nominally as a British commissioner, but in reality as an ally of the three American commissioners.

Gourley even argued that Alverstone was "appointed . . . with instructions, in the interest of the empire, to give the award that he has given."[5] Even Laurier remonstrated that this accusation was incredible though it contained some truth. Because Alverstone did not protest against these accusations but took refuge in his honour as a British judge, it is no accident that Canadians have regarded him as a traitor, not only to his oath as a commissioner and judge but also to his word as an English gentleman. His actions seemed to follow the pattern of British policy towards Canada. Perhaps the islands lost were small, but the principle of of British sacrifice of a "Canadian asset . . . to pander to United States goodwill to England," complained the Ottawa *Journal* on October 21, 1903, was not "small." Writing to the London *Economist* on November 2, 1903, its Ottawa correspondent reported that a

> high official of the Dominion Government has said: — 'Like animals doomed to vivisection for the benefit of science, Canada has been operated on unsparingly for the good of the Empire.'[6]

Once more the grim ritual of Canada's sacrifice on the altar of Anglo-American friendship seemed humiliatingly re-enacted.

The apparent failure of the British press to understand Canada's outrage and the "unconscious condescension" of Englishmen intensified anti-British sentiment. When Canada was called upon to play the game, the Montreal *Herald* retorted on October 22,1903, "But has the game been fairly played?"[7] The obtuseness of the British press was, however, exaggerated; much of it sympathized with Canada's loss.

Indications confirm what Minto asserted, that the intensity of Canadian feelings did not find full expression in the press. Alexander Muir, author of "The Maple Leaf Forever," and principal of a Toronto public school, "having read the news of the sacrifice of Canada's rights in the Alaska Boundary," obtained permission of the Chairman of the Toronto Board of Education on Trafalgar Day, October 21, to put the flag at half mast.[8] A British Columbia audience booed the singing of "God Save the King," and for the word betray Canadians coined the term "alverstonize."

The Canadian Government sought to fix the blame on Britain by publishing selected Alaska Boundary correspondence. This demonstrated that, while Canada was protesting American appointments, Britain had exchanged ratifications without Canada's consent. The House of Commons debate also tended to fix the blame on Britain, in spite of Henri Bourassa's trenchant analysis of Canadian contentions. As a former secretary of the Joint High Commission and privy to information not generally known Bourassa concluded that "Great Britain would not have any right whatever to the inlets that penetrated the coast." So devastating was his analysis that S. E. Gourley broke in

> Has the hon. gentleman a brief from Washington? Does he think that in this British parliament he is called upon to argue a case that has been ably argued from the American side by paid advocates from Washington?

The Conservative leader, Robert Borden, later also doubted that the Canadian case was "so absolutely absurd and ridiculous as he would lead us to believe." However most Canadian experts, whether Liberals like Bourassa, Goldwin Smith, or Adam Shortt or imperialists like R. E. Gosnell or Colonel Denison, considered Canada's case weak. The alternative to Canada's bad legal case, Bourassa continued, was compromise. And if Britain in the defence of her world-wide interests was right in sacrificing Canadian interests, Canada should similarly look after her own interests. She should deal with the United States not through the British Ambassador but through a Canadian agent.[9]

Although Laurier later in the debate naively complained of the United States as "very grasping," he realistically noted that Canada did not dare refuse assent to the Hay-Herbert Treaty. Refusal would probably have led Americans to plant their "flag upon the disputed territory" from which Canada would have had "to retire with disgrace, or go to war." This devastating disclosure was, however, quickly covered up by asserting that Canada's predicament resulted from Britain's withholding treaty-making powers from Canada. Laurier's disclosure of the *political* reality contradicted his claim that Canada lacked the *constitutional* powers. Of course Canada possessed the necessary constitutional powers in 1903, but it would have been suicidal to have exercised them. In raising the colonialist bogey successfully once more Laurier was balming Canada's soreness and excusing his refusal to use the political powers the government possessed. Sir Richard Cartwright, pro-American member of Laurier's cabinet, admitted to Lord Minto that it was partly a "red herring" useful for diverting attention from the "Alaska argument."[10] The Conservative press accused the Premier of drawing attention from the Canadian Government to Lord Alverstone and the British Government.

The Liberal press took up the cry of the need for treaty-making power. The *Globe* even accused the British Ambassador in Washington of acting as a "stool pigeon" for the United States in Canadian matters. This demand also made respectable and intensified talk of Canada's separation from Britain, for contemporary theory of sovereignty held that a state's rights to make treaties implied independence. Laurier denied the implication, but the Conservative press emphasized its validity. "Does any sane, sober-thinking Canadian doubt for a moment," warned the Conservative Ottawa *Citizen*, "that it is only the British flag that prevents the aggressive and greedy nation to the south of us from stripping us to the bone of all desirable territory."

Nevertheless the Canadian sense of outrage, particularly in Toronto, might have provided separatist leadership if Aylesworth had given a lead. At the Canadian Club banquet planned in his honour, there were rumours that Union Jacks would not deck the banquet hall nor "God Save the King" be sung. But nothing untoward happened. Aylesworth allayed Canadian feelings in a speech which, while critical of Alverstone, ended with a questioning peroration: Was it "not still a matter of . . . pride . . . to say . . . A British subject I was born, a British subject I will die?"[11]

THE REACTION OF MINTO, ALVERSTONE, AND THE BRITISH GOVERNMENT

Minto was dismayed by these developments. On October 25, 1903, he cabled the Colonial Office that Canadians assumed the decision was not "judicial. Feelings were very bitter in consequence. Publication of official statement that the case was decided on its merits urgently necessary."[12] With the concurrence of the Foreign Office the Colonial Office refused: it pointed to the published reasons. Nor was Minto officially supported when he defended the decision among Canadians, denying, for example, the strategic value of Sitklan and Kannaghunut. When Colonial Office officials proposed forwarding intelligence estimates on the strategic worthlessness of the two islands, Anderson was opposed:

> It is not a question of the value of the islands. What hurts is that we have, it is alleged wantonly sacrificed something belonging to Canada to placate or curry favour with the U.S. There is no getting over it; and the less we say the better.

For a time, too, Minto defended Lord Alverstone's conduct.

Meantime Alverstone, indignant at Canadian accusations and the exposure of the contradictions in his public explanation, unwisely engaged in correspondence with Aylesworth and Laurier. He took refuge in the integrity of British judges. Alverstone defended his conduct as judicial, a word which Canadians understood in the legal sense but which Alverstone used more in the sense of "judicious." He affirmed that he had made his judgment according to the evidence, and had he not agreed to the American contention as to the location of Portland Canal there would have been no agreement. Aylesworth, doubtless with the comparison of the breakdown of the Joint High Commission in mind, replied that he would have regarded such a result with equanimity. But the more Alverstone defended himself, the more the accusation of his having made a diplomatic decision seemed true. Minto therefore wrote to Alverstone for a refutation of Canadian charges in order to show the refutation privately to Canadians. But when the answer in effect confirmed Canadian charges Minto was indignant in his reply to Alverstone. Canada had suffered an injustice in the division of the islands.[13]

In a "confidential letter" on the same day (December 22, 1903), Laurier refuted Alverstone's judicial contentions. In the Portland Inlet the Canadian contention was "overwhelming." It "was simply a question of identity," founded on Vancouver's narrative, a contention Alverstone had admitted at the tribunal session of September 15. Secondly, how could the line in the Chilkat area be more judicial than the provisional line of October 20, 1899? Finally, since the tribunal's purpose was to make a settlement, how could a dangerous gap of 120 miles be left unsettled? Anderson commented: "Laurier's letter will take some answering on the part of the C.J."[14] But the poor Chief Justice could not publically affirm that he had been intimidated. This would have angered Roosevelt, and endangered Canada's and Britain's position.

So pessimistic was Minto at the state of Anglo-Canadian relations that he again strongly urged Britain to refute Canadian statements. Britain refused: it would not "likely serve any useful purpose." Minto sadly confessed to Chamberlain on December 14, 1903,

> The 'award' will be hoarded up with other supposed grievances, such as the Maine frontier story, &c. &c. always ready to be produced in proof of the want of sympathy of the Mother country.

With his usual penetration Chamberlain replied two weeks later (December 28, 1903):

My own belief is that Sir Wilfrid wanted to settle almost at any price, but he wanted at the same time to throw the blame of any concession on to our shoulders.[15]

Britain tried to get its case before the public by having telegrams supporting its position included in a British Blue Book and similar Canadian White Paper. Thus Minto several times pressed for the inclusion of the British answer of April 2, 1903, to the Canadian telegram of March 6, 1903, accusing Britain of a "serious departure from good faith" because of premature ratification. In that telegram Chamberlain had said that he understood that while Canada disliked the nominations the Dominion would not break off on that ground. Laurier agreed with Minto that the Government had decided to accept the treaty but that there was no reference in the correspondence to the Canadian Government's having accepted "impartial jurists" and the dispatch implied that they had done so. While Laurier's ground for the exclusion of this telegram seems to have some validity his argument for the exclusion of Lansdowne's telegram of July 16, 1902 to A. S. Raikes (the chargé at Washington) containing a report of Laurier's request of Choate for a boundary settlement were specious. Minto reported that Laurier "most positively" objected to its inclusion. While Laurier admitted meeting Choate two or three times he claimed that he had forgotten the subjects of the conversations. If the boundary question did come up Choate did not "rightly apprehend" Laurier's remarks. Minto angrily commented to Lansdowne, "Of course his conversation with Choate absolutely stultified him in the line he wants to adopt on the Alaska business — viz., that he is let into the Tribunal by H. M. Govt. — wh. is sheer nonsense." Lansdowne agreed; Laurier's refusal was "very shabby."[16]

A month later the Canadian Government demanded publication of the whole correspondence since February, 1899, and particularly all the dispatches in relation to the "impartial jurists" and ratification. But the Foreign Office would not yield in publishing confidential material, as Laurier doubtless knew it would not. The *Canada Sessional Paper* (No. 46a), 1904, contained several important telegrams or parts thereof that were repetitions of the one issued on the previous October 22, 1903.

It was not issued until July 8, 1904, late in the session when the issue was dead; and there was not even a debate in Parliament on the subject. It looks, therefore, as if the length of the argument over inclusions and exclusions was largely a charade.

Meanwhile in February, 1904, Lord Lansdowne defended the award in the British Parliament. He emphasized the unity of British and Canadian interests and observed that while it was not "expected" that Britain would win "all points" he was inclined to find some consolation in the fact that the two islands lost were of "no strategical value whatever." While a student may agree with A. E. Campbell's harsh comment on the implication of Lansdowne's statement that while Britain had lost some points she had gained others as "sheer dishonesty,"[17] nevertheless he was Foreign Secretary, responsible for the interests of Britain and the British Empire including Canada, and unable to forget the British Empire's declining position in a world of emerging new naval powers — United States, Germany, and Japan.

Of the three countries involved in the Alaska boundary dispute Britain's policy was the least Machiavellian and the most intelligent. Long aware of the weakness of Canada's Alaska boundary case and her fatuous blindness to the realities of power, she had to accommodate herself to the growing might of the United States. Britain succeeded in maintaining United States friendship, and both Canada and the United States participated in World Wars I and II.

CANADA AND AMERICAN IMPERIALISM

Canada's outrage against Alverstone was accentuated by outrage and helplessness against the United States. John W. Foster was alarmed at this mood. Writing apprehensively to Sifton on October 23, 1903, he hoped that Canadians would "soon get over their disappointment. We have too much in common to be other than the best of friends, and you and I must do all we can to make & keep them such." Sifton provided reassurances, but by December 9 Sifton was observing to J. W. Dafoe that the United States was "going to be the biggest bully the world had ever seen." Within a week of the award Canada's dread was

strikingly shown in a comment of the Montreal *Herald*:
"Teacher: Describe Canada. Pupil: Canada is that portion of
North America the United States doesn't want." In quoting this
observation the *Literary Digest* remarked that it "not inaptly
summed up" Canadian press opinion.[18]

Fantasy laments at Canada's failure to purchase Alaska were
mingled with fears for Canada's future. Canadian leaders and
the Canadian press called on Canada to enter negotiations at
once for the union of Newfoundland with Canada, for the
acquisition of St. Pierre and Miquelon from France, and even
Greenland from Denmark. Canada was enjoined to look to the
security of its Arctic archipelago, and of Hudson Bay where
American whalers and poachers were active. In fact even before
the Alaska award was made, the Canadian Government on
August 13, 1903, had authorized an expedition to Hudson Bay,
ostensibly for scientific purposes, but in reality to assert sovereignty, a purpose which soon became an open secret.

The American press took an intense interest in Canada's reaction to the award. It lavished praise on Alverstone's "judicial"
decision, though Roosevelt had indiscreetly praised it as "diplomatic." The New York *Times* repudiated Canadian aspersions
on Alverstone's judicial integrity as "simply incredible." The
American Law Review stigmatized the accusation as a "gross
offense against propriety and decency." On the contrary, it
asserted that Canada had received more than it deserved, an
opinion shared by many Americans. In defending the American
award the *Law Review* confused the Prince of Wales Island
with Wales Island and had Canada occupying Dyea, Skagway,
and Juneau, from each of which under the award Canada had
to withdraw![19] Such gross factual errors in this quarter suggest
blind trust among Americans rather than wide knowledge of the
Alaska question.

But the predominant note of the American press was ridicule
and contempt for Canada's sulk. Canadians were depicted as
"childish," "babyish," and "peevish"; their policy of "nag and
bicker" had failed. The Chicago *Record-Herald* caricatured
Mother England administering a bottle to squalling Canada and
trying to pacify the baby with "There! There! Don't cry! Just
See! What a Pretty Bottle for Baby!" Even Hay wrote to his wife
on October 23, 1903, that though he did not "wonder" why

Canada was "furious," yet he added "as Will Thomson used to say 'Serves 'em right, they can't take a joke.' "[20] Ambassador Choate betrayed the same insensitivity to the defeated when he suggested at the Guildhall Banquet of November 9, 1903, that a mountain on the new boundary be named "Mt. Herbert." Lansdowne wrote to Minto that this suggestion was "invented for an after-dinner speech," and was, according to Alfred Lyttleton, Chamberlain's successor, "received with icy silence."[21]

Exactly two weeks after the Alaska award on November 3, 1903, the Panama revolution occurred. The recognition of the new republic by the United States two days later intensified anti-Americanism in Canada. This time the sequence of events, including the United States' prevention of Colombia's putting down the revolution, made it impossible for the Canadians to deny the circumstantial involvement of the Roosevelt administration in the Panama revolution and its implications for the Alaska award and for the future of Canada. A Vancouver audience hissed the Stars and Stripes and forced the bringing down of the curtain. In Montreal an audience "began to yell and hoot" at the American flag and sang "God Save the King" to the end.[22] The flag was also hissed in Ottawa.

With Americans transferring their interest from Canada to the "cooked-up Republic," Canadians could now safely echo and intensify the moral outrage of Roosevelt's opponents. The Canadian press relished the New York *Journal-Posts's* acid comment, "Who could have imagined than an American Administration would make the Jameson Raid look respectable?" Even the Toronto *Globe*, which studiously avoided the implications of the Panama revolution for Canada, had to admit the sharp practice of the United States. Professor McGregor Young of the University of Toronto speaking on November 10, 1903, at the inaugural dinner of the Ottawa Canadian Club on the Monroe Doctrine pointed out the change in its nature from a policy of a right to independence to its existing "grasping policy." The Toronto *Star* observed that "the Monroe Doctrine may protect us against everybody but the United States but who will protect us against the United States." The mood of fear was well summed up in a Montreal *Star* cartoon, reproduced in the *Literary Digest,* entitled "American Aggression." It pictured an American eagle as a vulture scanning the horizon from a hilltop, with John Bull asleep on a distant island and the bones of "Alaska" and "Panama" close by. The "American Eagle" croaks out: "Let me see; what else is there in sight now?"[23]

AMERICAN AGGRESSION.

AMERICAN EAGLE—"Let me see; what else is there in sight now?"

Courtesy of the Montreal *Star*

The government also was angry and afraid. Sir Richard Cart-wright on November 13, 1903, informed Minto that Laurier had already had "to restrain a party in the Cabinet violently hostile to the U.S. who were ready to rush into extreme measures at once in the direction of commercial retaliation and prohibitory Tariffs." On December 3, 1903, Laurier gave Minto a "secret" Cabinet memorandum for Britain on the subject of United States threats to Canada, which began:

> It has long been apparent in those who have noted the trend of events in the United States that the most popular policy in the Republic is the extension of its territory.

Canadians could not forget that a big part of the territory west of the Great Lakes "orginally formed part of Canada as ceded by France to Great Britain. The public men and the press" look to the time that the "natural destiny" of Canada would be to be part of the United States.

> In view of those sentiments it is obviously in the interests of the Empire that no additional territory should be acquired by the United States in or adjacent to the north half of the continent of North America.

It concluded by warning of threats to Canada's Arctic and Den-mark's Greenland. Canada's immediate protection was the United States' need for Britain's co-operation in a prospective Russo-Japanese War.

In spite of Canada's well-founded fears United States pressure relaxed. Having given Canada the lesson it needed the United States was now disposed to be relatively generous. In the next eight years American officials made "Pilgrimages to Ottawa"[24] seeking agreements with a cool Canada. Accordingly in January, 1904, Hay unoffcially inquired when Canada would appoint officials to help demarcate the Alaska boundary. Canada made no delays, and Laurier welcomed, too, a Foreign Office sug-gestion that the two Commissioners should also demarcate the 120-mile gap. He warily suggested, however, that the United States officially make these proposals first. Hay obliged, and further suggested that the demarcation of the 141st meridian be also proceeded with. Sifton recommended that the latter suggestion should be carried out by special convention. Hay was sympathetic, but to avoid the "risk [of] rousing controversy," refused. In 1906, however, Congress passed a convention authorizing a geodetic survey of the 141st meridian. Meanwhile the two Commissioners, W. F. King and O. H. Tittmann, appointed to demarcate the Alaska Panhandle boundary, made joint recommendations, which were officially approved by an exchange of notes on March 25, 1905.[25]

ESTIMATE OF THE UNITED STATES PART IN THE ALASKA BOUNDARY QUESTION

The United States had the better case, the superior diplomatic skill, and the greater power to ensure victory. When a negotiator has all the aces, the power and skill to impose his will, and the will to use that power — if necessary, not too scrupulously — it is difficult to lose. The United States was angry at Canada's gall in challenging an unchallenged treaty. Canadians were often regarded as provincial bumpkins, and naive bumpkins as well. Although Canada had modelled itself after the United States in its political and economic structure, for it to engage in "Gargantuan diplomacy",[26] inflated by dreams of national grandeur, was to court trouble.

The trouble began in the 1880s when Justice Gray and the Executive Council of British Columbia began challenging the map line that Russia had asserted in 1826. Had the claims been strictly in accordance with the treaty and without grandiose inflation, and negotiations conducted with strict awareness of United States power in North America, it is conceivable that Canada's negotiations might have proceeded better than they did. Joseph Hunter's line on the Stikine River accepted by the United States in 1878 had been a relative Canadian success. But inflated Canadian claims could not withstand the aggressive nationalism of the United States in the 1890s, which in effect included interference in Canadian territory — in the Yukon. In spite of Canada's failure to induce the United States to compromise, Canadians would not admit that Anglo-Canadian power in North America was much less than that of the United States.

Canada's uncompromising policy hardened United States policy. But the final boundary settlement was delayed by the Boer War. As Britain's unofficial ally in the Boer War the United States administration avoided embarrassment in Alaska, though it took advantage of Britain's preoccupation to gain the right of building an Isthmian canal. Thus the prospect of a bargain concerning Alaska, which had really only existed in Canadian minds, had gone. The Boer War had also exposed the British Empire's weaknesses and undermined Britain's diplomatic influence. Most decisive in the final award was the advent of the ruthless Roosevelt, who believed that Canada did not have a leg to stand on in the Alaska boundary question. He finally agreed to a settlement on conditions that Hay had insisted upon, which guaranteed that the United States could not lose. In analyzing Canada's contemptuous treatment in the negotiations, J. W. Dafoe was particularly incensed at Roosevelt's part in the boundary settlement. But as Senator Lodge observed to President Roosevelt: "Canada is in that worst of all possible positions of possessing power unaccompanied by any responsibility."[27] The support from Americans that Roosevelt received in that settlement and in the subsequent Panama revolution shows that the President voiced the sentiment of most Americans. But the ruthlessness of his actions left a heritage of Canadian bitterness, which Canadians hid from themselves by blaming Britain.

THE GREAT EVASION: CANADA BLAMES BRITAIN FOR THE ALASKA AWARD

Laurier was chiefly responsible for the Alaska award, though there were extenuating circumstances. He inherited extreme claims and was politically committed to support the point of view of the provinces — in this case British Columbia; initially he lacked diplomatic experience and as a Canadian trusted in improvisation and Britain's diplomatic power and skill, instead of developing Canadian expertise. He miscalculated Britain's power in North America, for like nearly all Canadians he failed to see the implications of the Venezuela Incident. Nor is he to be criticized too severely for exploiting and becoming a prisoner of a potent anti-American mood, which was made popular, and was masked by, Imperial unity. Obviously too, a Prime Minister must handle anti-Americanism in Canada with care.

What is unforgivable in a statesman is the pursuit of unnecessary and unpopular pro-American policies, from which he could not escape. Even worse, as a student of President Lincoln and consequently of the power of the North in the Civil War, Laurier had no reason to underestimate the strength of the United States or its aggressive nationalism. He was blinded by his friendship ideology for the United States, liberalism, and belief in the power of treaty right. To inveigle the United States into entering the Joint High Commission; to confront its delegates initially with extreme Alaska claims vulnerable to the damaging charge of a recent Canadian invention; and to break off negotiations on the ground of United States failure to agree to Canadian boundary contentions, when other matters under negotiation had been virtually agreed upon, was to court disaster. Nor could the Conservative party's support of the government's position prevent Canada's defeat in the *modus vivendi* of October 20, 1899: Canadian territory was blocked from the sea. Enthusiasm for participation in the Boer War hid this defeat from the Canadian public.

But by the end of 1899 Laurier, warned by now that Britain would not support extreme boundary claims, must have known that Canada would lose. Accordingly his problem was to save Canada's face and his government's. By saddling an external body with the boundary decision, the decision could appear to be *imposed* on Canada, and would also successfully conceal his own inept policies. Fortunately for the existence of the Laurier Government the naive advice of Herbert and the fears and the exasperation of the British Foreign Office at Canada's dilatory action in approving the Hay-Herbert Treaty in 1903, led it into technically unconstitutional actions. Laurier seized on those actions to blame Britain. Sifton, supported by Laurier, also took advantage of the anger of the Canadian Commissioners in London and of Britain's necessities to blame Lord Alverstone for Canada's failures in the tribunal. Although the Canadian public had many grounds for sensing that the United States bore considerable responsibility for the decision, Canada maintained the pretence of Britain's responsibility. It manoeuvred Britain into withholding documents that would largely have exonerated Britain. But Britain dared not expose the pretence because of danger to its own position.

Of course succeeding Canadian Governments have a vested interest in maintaining the pretence. But why has the Canadian public not accepted the fact that the Alaska boundary decision was dictated by the United States? As early as May 25, 1911, John W. Foster disclosed President Roosevelt's "first" intention of occupying the disputed territory by force. Ever since, a series of disclosures have revealed more and more of the story so that in academic circles at least Roosevelt's "big-stick" policy is well known. But United States policy for the 1903 decision and its pressures on Canada in the era 1896-1903 have never been accepted generally by Canadians.

Why not? The Alaska boundary dispute certainly puts the United States in a bad light and Canada in a worse light. Canada's unwise and jingo policies were compounded by Laurier's and Sifton's Machiavellianism. The fact was Canada had received a brutal, and to a considerable extent a deserved, lesson in power politics. Canada had good reason to be afraid for its future. It could no longer hide behind the mantle of colonialism because the motherland had been exposed as weak and apparently untrustworthy. Canada clothed her fearfulness in a return to her traditional American model. Although Canada in 1867 had modelled itself in many ways after the United States, it was obvious in 1903 that the twentieth century would not belong to Canada. But Canadians could symbolically belong to the world of twentieth century Americans: they could accept the American projection on themselves as potential Americans. To treat themselves as potential Americans, however, was to undermine their confidence in their own country and to undergo periodic fits of frustration and self-recrimination as they measured Canadian institutions and practices by inappropriate American standards.

In spite of many similarities, Canada differs in fundamentals from the United Sates. Canada is a bi-racial state, is rooted in an unrevolutionary past, and dwells in a harsh environment. It possesses an intellectual tradition characterized by "recognition of human limitation, the awareness of ambiguity and the urge to communicate."[28] Canada does not fit the universal ideology of the Declaration of Independence with its eighteenth-century certainties of inherent rights and revolution, reason and the importance of the type. Difference, not similarity, is an essence of Canada. Canada's primary roots lie not in classical but in Christian experience — in the predominantly Christian and traditional experience of seventeenth-century France and nineteenth-century Britain. Individual uniqueness is important, and the maintenance of racial and regional differences is inherent in the nature of Canadian experience.

This does not mean that Canada is any better or any worse than the United States: it is simply different. In a world of crushing similarity and boring impersonality, uniqueness and difference can give meaning to life. If the continued existence of Canada is regarded as a good thing — and by their recent actions Canadians believe so — differences should be cherished. But before they can be cherished their value must be accepted. After decades of denial this will be painful, and nowhere more so than in an acceptance of all the ramifications of the Alaska boundary question. But it would be a good place to begin.

Notes

Chapter 1

1. For an account of early Russian explorations and the fur trade, see Alfred Hulse Brooks, "History of Explorations and Surveys," in Morgan B. Sherwood, ed., *Alaska and Its History* (Seattle and London, University of Washington Press, 1967), pp. 21-44. *Alaska and Its History* contains other useful essays bearing on the Alaska Boundary question.

2. The text of the Ukase will be found in the Appendix to the United States Case, *Proceedings of the Alaskan Boundary Tribunal*, 58th Cong. 2nd Sess., Sen. doc. no. 162 (Ser. nos. 4600-6 and atlases) (Washington, 1904), vol. II, pp. 23-25. Hereafter this document will be cited as *A.B.T.*, vol. I, etc.

3. For an account of Yankee traders on the Pacific, relevant chapters will be found in S. E. Morison, *The Maritime History of Massachusetts 1783-1860* (Boston, Houghton Mifflin, 1921) and Raymond A. Rydell, *Cape Horn to the Pacific* (Berkeley and Los Angeles, University of California Press, 1952), chap. II, "The Old China Trade." The quoted comment is from Henry Middleton to John Q. Adams, April 7/19, 1824, *A.B.T.* vol. II, p. 77. As many of the letters written from Russia referred to in this chapter have this double date, an explanation is called for. The first date, April 7, 1824, is the date according to the Julian Calendar, which was the calendar used in Russia and in countries where

the Orthodox Church flourished. The second date, April 19, 1824, twelve days later, is the equivalent date according to the Gregorian Calendar, which most of the world follows.

4. The texts will be found in *A.B.T.*, vol. II, pp. 25-28. An Italian mile is 6085.2 feet. The Russians based their maritime exclusion on a provision in the Anglo-French Treaty of Utrecht, 1713-14, which forbade French vessels approaching Nova Scotia closer than thirty leagues southwest of Sable Island. On the decline of seal rookeries compare Raymond A. Rydell: "The history of any seal rookery was the same: one, discovery of the sealing ground; two, indiscriminate slaughter of young and old seals alike; three, no seals; four, no hunters," (*op. cit.*, p. 36). For useful historical sketches see "Drawing the Alaskan Boundary," by Stuart R. Tompkins, originally appearing March, 1945, *Can. Hist. Rev.*, and reprinted in Sherwood, *op. cit.*, pp. 83-112 and John S. Galbraith, *The Hudson's Bay Company as an Imperial Factor 1821-1869* (Berkeley and Los Angeles, Univ. of Calif. Press, 1957), ch. 6, and pp. 177-81.

5. For the Convention of 1818 see A. L. Burt, *The United States, Great Britain and British North America* (New Haven, Yale, 1940), chap. XVIII and S. F. Bemis *John Quincy Adams and the Foundations of American Foreign Policy* (New York, Knopf, 1949), pp. 280-90; on the Spanish Treaty see also

Bemis, *op. cit.*, chs. XV, XVI.
6. Bemis, *op. cit.*, chs. XVII, XVIII, XIX; and Frederick Merk, *Albert Gallatin and the Oregon Problem* (Cambridge, Harvard, 1950), chs. II and III.
7. *A.B.T.*, vol. II, pp. 144-49.
8. *Ibid.*, pp. 153-66, C. Bagot to George Canning, March 17/29, 1824.
9. Text of the treaty in *ibid.*, pp. 8-12; an account of the negotiations will be found in H. Middleton to J. Q. Adams, April 7/19, 1824, *ibid.*, pp. 69-80; quotation from Bemis, *op. cit.*, p. 523.
10. *A.B.T.*, vol. II, pp. 175-208.
11. *Ibid.*, p. 179, Lieven to Nesselrode, May 20/June 1, 1824; Canning's quotation *ibid.*, p. 209.
12. Version of the treaty from *British and Foreign State Papers, 1824-1825* (London, James Ridgway & Sons, 1846), pp. 38-43, *A.B.T.*, vol. II, pp. 14-16, and John A. Munro, *The Alaska Boundary Dispute* (Toronto, Copp Clark, 1970), pp. 9-10. An account of the final negotiations is in Stratford Canning to George Canning, Feb. 1/13, 1825, *A.B.T.*, vol. II, pp. 212-24.
13. Map in Hon. J. W. Foster, "The Alaskan Boundary," *Nat. Geog. Mag.*, vol. X (Nov. 1899), p. 437. See map on p. 13. Quotation in Lieven to Nesselrode, May 8/20, 1825, *A.B.T.* vol. II, p. 230.
14. A useful reference to the maps will be found in Charles Callan Tansill, *Canadian-American Relations 1875-1911* (Toronto, Ryerson, 1943), pp. 127-28.
15. Galbraith, *op. cit.*, pp. 146-55.
16. Tansill, *op. cit.*, p. 129.

Chapter 2
1. The text of the treaty is in *Alaskan Boundary Tribunal* (58th Cong., 2nd Sess., Senate doc., 162), vol. II, pp. 17-22.

2. For a description of the geography and the resources of the Alaska Panhandle see F. W. Gibson, *The Alaskan Boundary Dispute* (Master's thesis, Queen's University, 1944), pp. 1-6; on the political, economic, and social conditions in Alaska in the early days of United States authority, see *ibid.*, pp. 70-73, 88-91 and Ted. C. Hinckley, "Sheldon Jackson and Benjamin Harrison," in Morgan B. Sherwood, *Alaska and its History* (Seattle and London, Univ. of Wash. Press, 1967), pp. 293-312.
3. Charles C. Tansill, *Canadian-American Relations 1875-1911* (Toronto, Ryerson, 1943), pp. 131-32; and cf. John A. Munro, *The Alaska Boundary Dispute* (Toronto, Copp Clark, 1970), p. 11.
4. F. W. Howay, W. N. Sage, and H. F. Angus, *British Columbia and the United States* (Toronto, Ryerson, 1942), pp. 365-68.
5. Tansill, *op. cit.*, pp. 135-36.
6. *Ibid.*, pp. 136-38.
7. *Ibid.*, p. 132.
8. *Ibid.*, pp. 139-41 and "Alaska Boundary Question," Report of . . . the Executive Council of British Columbia, *British Columbia Sessional Papers, 1885*, pp. 451-60. For the maps showing the growth of Canadian claims, see above, pp. 26-29.
9. Tansill, *op. cit.*, p. 141.
10. Cited in Robert Craig Brown, *Canada's National Policy 1883-1900* (Princeton Univ. Press, 1964), pp. 287-89.
11. FO Conf. Print 5439, p. 42, Alaska Boundary Correspondence, Part I (1886) [Copy in Univ. of Tor. Lib.], D. R. Cameron to Earl Granville, March 31, 1886, inc. in C.O. to F.O., April 8, 1886 and Brown *op. cit.*, pp. 289-91. The writer owes an apology to Mr. H. George Classen in the review of his *Thrust and*

122

Counterthrust (Toronto, Long-mans, 1965) in the *Can. Hist. Rev.*, vol. XLVIII (Spring 1967), p. 68, in which he was skeptical of Mr. Classen's emphasis on Cameron's influence on subsequent British and Canadian interpretations of the Alaska boundary question. Mr. Classen was right and the writer was wrong.

12. *A.B.T.*, British Atlas, Map 25, Memorandum on the face of the map by W. J. I., Wharton, Hydrographer, April 17, 1886.

13. U. of T. FO Conf. Print 5439, p. 48, Memorandum of D. R. Cameron, April 9, 1886, inc. in C.O. to F.O., "Confidential," April 14, 1886 and *ibid.*, p. 63, Memorandum of D. R. Cameron, July 14, 1886, inc. in C.O. to F.O., "Conf.," July 27, 1886.

14. J. A. S. Grenville, *Lord Salisbury and Foreign Policy* (London, Athlone Press (Univ. of Lon.), 1964), p. 58.

15. Brown, *op. cit.*, pp. 291-93 and Tansill, *op. cit.* p. 154. Dall asserted that he and Dawson agreed that the conference was informal.

16. Histories of the United States give accounts of this incident. Sackville-West has received too much blame by Canadians for the vagueness of his inquiry of the Secretary of State concerning a Canadian complaint. He omitted completely the details that "a Charter is about to be granted by the Alaskan authorities of the United States for certain privileges in that part of Alaska which is claimed by this country." Thus Canada lost an opportunity—probably fortunately—of making a specific claim on Lynn Canal. But Sackville-West's vague letter to T. F. Bayard is virtually a *verbatim* copy of Lord Salisbury's letter to Sackville-West (Aug. 31, 1888, FO Conf. Print, 5774, *op. cit.* pp. 12-14).

17. Brown, *op. cit.*, pp. 294-95 and FO Conf. Print, 5774, pp. 20-21 (A. B. Corres. Part III) in F.O. to C.O., Dec. 6, 1888, and Tansill, *op. cit.* p. 157.

18. U of T FO Conf. Print, 6055, pp. 9-11 (A.B. Corres. Part IV), Memorandum of Min. of Interior, Feb. 25, 1889, becoming Minute of Council, June 30, 1890, inc. in C.O. to F.O., Aug. 22, 1890. Reference to "incognito" in *ibid.* p. 12, Otto J. Klotz to A. M. Burgess, Dep. Min. of Interior, Dec. 1, 1889.

19. Brown, *op. cit.*, pp. 296-97.

20. *Ibid.*, pp. 297-98.

21. The Joint Report of the "Alaska Boundary Commission" without maps is in *Can. Sess. Pap.* (No. 74) 1896.

Chapter 3

1. The subject of these two paragraphs is the basic theme of Norman Penlington, *Canada and Imperialism 1896-1899* (Univ. of Tor. Press, 1965).

2. For a lively account of the Yukon Gold Rush, see Pierre Berton, *The Klondike Fever* (New York, Knopf, 1958).

3. The "open door" was a phrase usually applied to describe areas, subject to a single nationalist or imperialist influence or authority, kept open for the trade, investment, etc., of all nations. Its use here means that the United States exercised its power to create conditions enforcing equality for all miners, that is, American miners, entering the Yukon. See "The Open Door in the Yukon," in Penlington, *op cit.*, Chapter 7.

4. Penlington, *op. cit.*, pp. 82-90.

5. Robert Craig Brown, *Canada's National Policy 1883-1900* (Princeton Univ. Press, 1964), pp. 303-14; Penlington, *op. cit.*,

pp. 90-94; Charles S. Campbell, Jr., *Anglo-American Understanding, 1898-1903* (Baltimore, Johns Hopkins, 1957), pp. 72-73.

6. C. S. Campbell, Jr., *op. cit.,* p. 144, n. 24.

7. PAC Klotz Papers, Alaska Boundary, vol. 9, note on copy of O. J. Klotz to Laurier, September 28, 1898. Note also Laurier refused to see Klotz in Quebec because Klotz did not bring back evidence from St. Petersburg, which he had been sent for, in order to support the Canadian case. Klotz had not found a "treaty map. . . . They can choke me off but not truth & facts, which they will be forced to face before the matter is settled." (*ibid.*)

8. Authority for this action may have come from General Order No. 6, Feb. 18, 1898, of the Military Department of the Columbia, headquarters in State of Washington, issued by the local Assistant Adjutant General: "With the approval of the Acting Secretary of War" there was to be established a military district "embracing Lynn Canal . . . extending to the International Boundary and within fifty miles in other directions." NA R. G. 94, Gen. Orders and Circulars, Dept. of Columbia, vol. 170.

9. Brown, *op. cit.,* pp. 334-36 and Penlington, *op. cit.,* p. 101.

10. Brown, *op. cit.,* pp. 340-47.

11. C. S. Campbell, Jr., *op. cit.* p. 105 uses word "neglected." For accounts of the Alaska boundary question at the Joint High Commission see *ibid.,* pp. 102-119, Brown, *op. cit.,* pp. 378-91, and Penlington, *op. cit.,* pp. 123-31.

12. To Lord Salisbury, R. F. V. Heuston, *Lives of the Lord Chancellors 1885-1940* (Oxford, Clarendon Press, 1964), p. 125. In view of the nationalistic state of public opinion on both sides if a leak had not occurred the storm would merely have been postponed. On the other hand if Chamberlain was responsible his action throws a sinister light on his attempts to manipulate Canadian public opinion to ensure Canada's participation in the Boer War.

13. On the breakdown see Penlington, *op. cit.,* pp. 125-31, C. S. Campbell, Jr., *op. cit.,* pp. 384-91.

14. Penlington, *op. cit.,* pp. 207, 198-203.

15. *Ibid.,* pp. 213-25.

16. *Ibid.,* pp. 208-9.

17. *Ibid.,* pp. 203-6, 209-10, Brown, *op. cit.,* pp. 391-96, and C. S. Campbell, Jr., *op. cit.,* ch. 6.

18. Penlington, *op. cit.,* pp. 210-11. Canada of course knew far less about the question that the Colonial Office did. Joseph Pope's pathetic letter to John Anderson to borrow "elementary papers" from the Colonial Office because Alaska boundary documents lay scattered in Ottawa government offices underscores that opinion. (PAC Pope Papers, vol. 49, f. 1, p. 18, July 10, 1899. "We sadly lack system here," he explained (*ibid.*).

19. C. S. Campbell, Jr., *op. cit.,* pp. 144-46, Penlington, *op. cit.,* pp. 210-12, and Brown, *op. cit.,* pp. 394-96.

20. Penlington, *op. cit.,* pp. 212-13, 237-38; Choate's latter dispatch is in *Alaskan Boundary Tribunal,* vol. IV (Ser. No. 4602), pp. 138-55 and *Can. Sess. Pap.* (No. 46a), 1904, pp. 11-25.

21. To Henry White, May 29, 1899, Charles C. Tansill, *Canadian-American Relations 1874-1911* (Toronto, Ryerson, 1943), p. 195.

Chapter 4

1. Roosevelt to Elihu Root, Aug. 8, 1903, Charles C. Tansill, *Canadian-American Relations 1874-1911* (Toronto, Ryerson, 1943), p. 246.
2. George E. Foster used this phrase positively in *Debates,* July 31, 1899, p. 8995, cited in Norman Penlington, *Canada and Imperialism 1896-1899* (Univ. of Tor. Press, 1965), p. 222.
3. PAC Sifton Papers, vol. 276, Colonial Office, North American, No. 187, p. 48, October 1899, "Confidential."
4. *Ibid.,* "Memorandum on the Boundary between Canada and Alaska in the Region of the Lynn Canal," Revise Colonial Office, North American, No. 185, October 1899. Quotations on p. 19. On page 1 in J. Pope's handwriting there appears: "Private. Given to me in London Oct. 1899. J. Pope."
5. Penlington, *op. cit.,* pp. 238-39 and 205-6. Neither of the basic American or Canadian contentions remained secret from the public, for two quasi-official articles appeared: John W. Foster delivered a lecture in Washington on "The Alaskan Boundary," *Nat. Geog. Mag.,* vol. X (Nov. 1899), pp. 424-56 with 12 pages of maps; and John A. Munro, *The Alaska Boundary Dispute* (Toronto, Copp Clark, 1970), pp. 12-14. Six months later *The Edinburgh Review,* vol. 192 (April 1900), pp. 279-304 contained an anonymous article attempting to answer Foster's speech and to set forth the Canadian case. It was written by Joseph Pope at the instance of Lord Minto, whose brother Arthur Elliot was editor of *The Edinburgh Review* (Pope Papers, vol. 49, p. 118, J. Pope to Arthur Elliot, Jan. 24, 1900).
6. Reported by Lord George Hamilton, Secretary for India, to Viscount Curzon, Viceroy of India, 4 July 1901, in G. W. Monger, *The End of Isolation British Foreign Policy, 1900-1907* (London, Nelson, 1963), p. 13; Monger's book (ch. I) contains a good description of Britain's weakening strategic position.
7. The theme of Professor Charles S. Campbell, Jr., *Anglo-American Understanding, 1898-1903* (Baltimore, Johns Hopkins, 1957) and A. E. Campbell, *Great Britain and the United States 1895-1903* (London, Longmans, 1960). "Black Week" refers to December 11 to December 16, 1899 when British armies received three serious checks from the Boers.
8. C. S. Campbell, Jr., *op. cit.,* ch. 9, "The Pauncefote Treaty."
9. Chamberlain to Minto, Jan. 30, 1900, *ibid.,* pp. 191-92. On Jan. 31, 1900, Laurier wrote to Minto, "We cannot but feel however that we are making a sacrifice, & giving up a considerable advantage, at least a tactical advantage." (PAC Minto Papers, vol. 7, p. 37.)
10. C. S. Campbell, Jr., *op. cit.,* chs. 9, 10.
11. *Ibid.,* ch. 11.
12. PAC CO 42/881, pp. 88-94 and U of T FO Conf. Print, 7576, A.B. Corres., 1900, Part XII, pp. 26-28, 35-36, 50-54 (Indians); and John Hay to Chairman, Committee of Miners, Porcupine Mining District, Alaska, Aug. 3, 1900 (*Foreign Relations 1899* (Washington, 1901), pp. 331-32).
13. Penlington, *op. cit.,* pp. 202-3; and PAC CO 42/876, pp. 97, 92, P.C. 186 L, May 29, 1900, inc. in Minto to Chamberlain, "Confidential," May 31, 1900.
14. PAC CO 42/890, p. 76, Lansdowne to Pauncefote, Jan. 23, 1902, inc. in FO Conf. Print to

C.O., Feb. 17, 1902; and *ibid.,* pp. 119-21, Hay to Pauncefote, Feb. 28, 1902, inc. in Pauncefote to Lansdowne, March 20, 1902, inc. in F.O. to C.O. April 8, 1902.

15. PAC Laurier Papers, pp. 40130-32, F. W. Vincent, Asst. Manager, Can. Pac. Navigation Co. to Laurier, Dec. 22, 1899. Commenting on the ruling in the Seattle *Post Intelligencer,* an American skipper observed: " 'Now we have an American Klondike, and its business should be held and done as far as possible by Americans in American ships. The Canadians treated us very unfairly in the matter of the Klondike,—drove Americans from Atlin and in every way sought to harass and discriminate against our people. They are simply getting what they deserve.' " *ibid.,* p. 40132, clipping. On shipping goods to the Yukon in this period see PAC CO 42/877, pp. 719-20; PAC F. C. Wade Papers, Alaska Boundary 1900-1942, undated penciled memorandum on difficulties of shipping goods; and for American complaints of Canadian practices see CO 42/878, pp. 610-612 and CO 42/885, pp. 763-68.

16. PAC CO 42/888, p. 321, P. C. March 14, 1902; cf. CO 42/882, pp. 573, 584, and CO 42/890, p. 235.

17. PAC F. C. Wade Papers, Alaska Boundary 1900-1942, vol. 1 (Memoranda and Notes, 1902-8) "Memo of practical inconveniences . . . of the N.W.M. Police, resulting from . . . the Alaska Boundary dispute." Ottawa, 10th October 1902, Sec. 5.

18. C. S. Campbell, Jr., *op. cit.,* pp. 230-44 and PAC CO 42/890, pp. 24-25.

19. PAC Laurier Papers, p. 61630, James Douglas, Jan. 22, 1902.

20. C. S. Campbell, Jr., *op. cit.,* pp.

188, 227-28; text of draft treaty in *Can. Sess. Pap.* (No. 46a), 1904, pp. 31-34.

21. U of T FO Conf. Print, pp. 33-34, A. B. Corres., XIII; PAC CO 42/884, p. 463 and cf. *ibid.,* p. 462, minute of H. B. Cox, "The Canadians are hopeless;" CO 42/883, pp. 555-56, Minto to Chamberlain, "Secret and Confidential," Aug. 24, 1901 paraphrase cable and FO Conf. Print, pp. 42-46, 47, Laurier to Minto, "Secret," Aug. 14, 1901, inc. Minto to Chamberlain, Aug. 23, 1901, inc. in C.O. to F.O., "Confidential," Sept. 14, 1901; PAC Laurier papers, pp. 215399-400, Chamberlain to Minto, "Secret," Sept. 19, 1901, paraphrase cable; Chamberlain quotation in PAC CO 42/877, p. 550, minute, Jan. 26, 1900.

22. Minto to Chamberlain, Oct. 15, 1901, cable, *Can. Sess. Pap.* (No. 46a), 1904, pp. 34-35 and *id.* to *id.,* Nov. 6, 1901, *ibid.,* pp. 33-37.

23. PAC Laurier Papers, pp. 215399-400, paraphrase "Secret," Sept. 19, 1901; "appeased" is Prof. Carman Miller's word, "Minto and Canadian-American Relations 1898-1904," typescript, p. 24, paper given at Can. Hist. Assoc. Meetings, June 1971.

24. T. Roosevelt to A. H. Lee (later Viscount Lee of Farham, former British military attaché in Washington), April 24, 1901, cited in Howard K. Beale, *Theodore Roosevelt and the Rise of America to World Power* (Baltimore, Johns Hopkins, 1956), p. 112; for a short analysis of Roosevelt's career, see John Morton Blum, *The Republican Roosevelt* (New York, Atheneum, 1967); for the Alaska boundary question after Roosevelt assumed power, see John A. Munro, *op. cit.,* part VI.

25. Beale, *op. cit.,* pp. 113-14 and

Report of the War Department, vol. IX, 1902, pp. 33, 38, 39 (House Doc. No. 2, 57th Congress, 2nd Sess. (No. 4451)).

26. C. S. Campbell, Jr., *op. cit.*, pp. 253-54, Pauncefote to Lansdowne, March 28, 1902.

27. Smalley to Laurier, probably Feb. 8, 1902 (PAC Laurier Papers, p. 61212); Kitson to Minto, March 26 (including memorandum), May 13, May 24, 1902 (PAC Minto Papers, vol. 21, pp. 198-201, 202, 205-8, respectively); Spring-Rice in Pope to Laurier, 21st May 1902, "Private and Confidential" (PAC Laurier Papers, pp. 65322-25). In May, 1902, Roosevelt told A. S. Raikes of the British Embassy that on the Alaska question he was "going to be ugly" (Lord Newton, *Lord Lansdowne* (London, Macmillan, 1929), p. 263); to Kitson in March, 1902, he used the word "nasty" (Minto Papers, vol. 21, p. 201).

28. PAC Minto Papers (C-3113), Packet No. 2, Notes of Conversations with Lord Minto and Sir Wilfrid Laurier 1902-1904, pp. 14-17, June 24, 1902.

29. PAC CO 42/890, pp. 246-47, Lansdowne to Arthur Raikes, June 25, 1902, inc. in F.O. to C.O., July 2, 1902.

30. Allan Nevins, *Henry White, Thirty Years of American Diplomacy* (New York, Harper, 1930), pp. 192-93, White to Hay, June 28, 1902.

31. Beale, *op. cit.*, pp. 115-16, and Choate to Hay, July 5, 1902, *John Hay, From Poetry to Politics* (New York, Dodd Mead, 1933), p. 457.

32. A. E. Campbell, *op. cit.*, pp. 109-10. This letter is in Munro, *op. cit.*, pp. 25-29. It is curious that the normally well-informed and astute Anderson should not have learned of Laurier's meeting with Choate until September 1,

1902, and that he did not discern the reason for what he called Laurier's "abject surrender" (*ibid.*, p. 38).

Chapter 5

1. John W. Dafoe, *Clifford Sifton* (Toronto, Macmillan, 1931), p. 217.

2. Allan Nevins, *Henry White,* (New York, Harper, 1930), pp. 224-25 and H. C. Lodge to Constance Lodge Gardner, Oct. 5, 1903, in John Garraty, "Henry Cabot Lodge and the Alaskan Boundary Tribunal," *New Eng. Quart.*, vol. 24 (Dec. 1951), p. 487.

3. "Pilgrimages to Ottawa: Canadian-American Diplomacy, 1903-14," *Historical Papers,* Can. Hist. Assoc., 1968, p. 66; Zara S. Steiner, *The Foreign Office and Foreign Policy, 1898-1914* (Camb. Univ. Press, 1969), p. 177 describes Herbert as "able."

4. Herbert to Minto, Oct. 16, 1902, "Private" (PAC Minto Papers, vol. 13, p. 10), and see *ibid.* for considerable correspondence between the two men.

5. C. S. Campbell, Jr., *Anglo-American Understanding, 1898-1903* (Baltimore, Johns Hopkins, 1957), p. 303; cf. also parts of *ibid.* quoted in John A. Munro, *The Alaska Boundary Dispute* (Toronto, Copp Clark, 1970), pp. 145-53.

6. C. S. Campbell, Jr., *op. cit.*, p. 306, n. 21.

7. Herbert to Minto, Jan. 19, 1903, telegram, *Can. Sess. Pap.* (No. 46a), 1904, p. 60; text of treaty in *ibid.*, pp. 55-59, Munro, *op. cit.*, pp. 41-43, and *A.B.T.*, vol. II, pp. 1-6.

8. Herbert to Lansdowne, Dec. 19, 1902, *Can. Sess. Pap.* (No. 46a), 1904, p. 54. Herbert reported that "if they exist" was added to the original draft.

9. PAC CO 42/892, p. 109, Minto to Onslow, "Secret & Confidential," decypher, Feb. 3, 1903 and *The Literary Digest,* XXVI (Feb. 14, 1903), pp. 235-36.

10. PAC Minto Papers (C-3115), vol. VII, p. 48, Laurier to Minto, Jan. 22, 1903 and A. E. Campbell, *Great Britain and the United States 1895-1903* (London, Longmans, 1960), p. 113, my emphasis.

11. Cypher from C.O. quoted in Minto to Herbert, Jan. 12, 1903 (PAC Minto Papers, Letter Book no. 3, (A-131), p. 342). The first hint is in Herbert to Lansdowne, Dec. 8, 1902 (*Can. Sess. Pap.* (No. 46a), 1904, p. 53). Even after the appointment of Root, Lodge, and Turner, Ambassador Herbert evidently failed to grasp the significance of their refusal to serve. "To sit on a 'diplomatic tribunal,' as they term it, would be incompatible with their positions as Members of the Supreme Court," he cabled to Lansdowne, "Secret", Feb. 14, 1903 (PRO FO 414/177, p. 17 (FO Conf. Print, 8296, A.B. Corres., XV)); Willard L. King, *Melville Weston Fuller Chief Justice of the United States 1888-1910* (New York, Macmillan, 1950), ch. XIX and Carman Miller, "Minto and Canadian-American Relations, 1898-1904," (typescript of paper given at Can. Hist. Assoc. meetings, 1971, p. 27).

12. In the original Hay-Pauncefote draft treaty of May 1901, the preamble referred to "arbitration" and the body spoke of an "arbitral tribunal." In December 1902 all references to "arbitration" or "arbitral" were removed by Senator Henry Cabot Lodge from the draft of the Hay-Herbert Treaty (C. C. Tansill, *Canadian-American Relations 1874-1911* (Toronto, Ryerson, 1943), p. 229) and the judicial body was simply called a "tribunal." Lodge also was evidently responsible for Hay's suggesting to Herbert on December 8 that the tribunal be called a "judicial commission." This sentence in the copy of Herbert's dispatch to Lansdowne that is in the Pope Papers (PAC) is underlined, but that sentence is omitted in the document as it appeared in the British blue book and the Canadian sessional papers. But by December 19 Herbert reported that Hay had dropped the suggestion of calling it a "judicial commission." Apparently sometime between December 19, 1902, and January 2, 1903, the word "arbitral" was reintroduced into the preamble before the word "tribunal." It was in this form that the treaty was signed on January 24, and printed by the Foreign Office and appeared in the *Canada Sessional Papers* for 1903 and 1904. But four days later the word "arbitral" was removed from the preamble, "without re-signing" a deletion Dennett calls a "significant 'correction'" (Tyler Dennett, *John Hay From Poetry to Politics* (New York, Dodd Mead, 1933), pp. 355-56). The corrected version is in *A.B.T.,* vol. II, pp. 1-6. Cf. also cables between Herbert and Lansdowne, Jan. 28, Jan. 30, and Feb. 2, 1903 (PRO FO 414/177, p. 10). The Foreign Office was irritated.

13. Lord Newton, *Lord Lansdowne* (London, Macmillan, 1929), p. 260 and PRO FO 5/2542, p. 85, for Lansdowne's undated comment on F. H. Villiers minute of Feb. 6, 1903.

14. A. E. Campbell, *Great Britain and the United States 1895-1903* (London, Longmans, 1960), p. 111. The account of the Hay-Herbert Treaty going through the Senate is from C. S. Campbell,

Jr., *op. cit.*, pp. 308-10. The Lodge comment is cited from John W. Dafoe *Clifford Sifton* (Toronto, Macmillan, 1931), p. 220, n.

15. John Charlton in *Globe,* Feb. 26, 1903, cited in J. Castell Hopkins, *Can. Ann. Rev., 1903* (Toronto, Can. Ann. Rev. Pub. Co., 1904), p. 352.

16. "Henry Cabot Lodge and the Alaska Boundary Award" by James White in "Notes and Documents," *Can. Hist. Rev.* vol. 6 (Dec. 1925), p. 334.

17. PAC Minto Papers, (C-3114), vol. XII, p. 60 to Rolly [Minto], "Private," Feb. 21, 1903; to Hay, "Private & Confidential", Feb. 24, 1903 (not "factious" as Tyler Dennett says in *John Hay* (New York, Dodd Mead, 1933), pp. 357-58); PAC Minto Papers, Letter Book no. 3 (A-131), pp. 399, 400, to Chamberlain, "Private," March 2, 1903; and *Can. Ann. Rev. 1903,* p. 356.

18. Lord Newton, *op. cit.,* p. 261 and PRO FO 414/177, p. 25, Onslow to Minto, postscript, "Secret and Personal," Feb. 18, 1903, inc. in C.O. to F.O., "Confidential," Feb. 20, 1903; *ibid.,* p. 25, C.O. to F.O., "Secret," Feb. 20, 1903; PRO FO 5/2542, p. 133, minute FHV (Villiers), Feb. 19, 1903.

19. *Can. Sess. Pap.* (No. 46a), 1904, p. 61, Minto to C.O. Feb. 19, and Feb. 21, 1903, cables. In the second cable the following was omitted from the sessional paper, without indication of an omission, "and on the further confidential assurance conveyed to me by Herbert that he had reason to" (continuing in published text, "hope that judges of the highest courts," etc.) (PAC CO 42/892, p. 153); and PRO FO 414/177, p. 25, C.O. to F.O., "Secret [and Immediate"], 20 Feb. 1903 and *ibid.,* p. 26, C.O. to F.O., "[Immediate and] Con-

fidential," 23 Feb. 1903. The Foreign Office omitted ["and Immediate (and)"] in its Conf. Print 8296.

20. PAC Minto Papers, Letter Book No. 3 (A-131), pp. 384-85, "Private," 19 Feb. 1903.

21. *Ibid.,* p. 391, Minto to Herbert, "Private," 25 Feb. 1903 and *passim*; see also *ibid.,* vol. I (C-3113), p. 33, Minto's conversations with Laurier, Feb. 26, 1903. There were no complaints that Herbert's mail and cables with England were being tampered with.

22. U. of T. John Charlton Papers, ms. Autobiography, pp. 967-68 and D-10-408, Diary, Feb. 20, 1903; PAC Pope Papers, vol. 55, f. 17, p. 165½, Herbert to Laurier, Feb. 22, 1903; PAC Minto Papers, vol. 13, pp. 26-27, March 30, 1903, and *ibid.,* p. 21, "Private," Feb. 23, 1903. As late as March 10, 1903, Herbert was writing to Lansdowne: "It is a somewhat remarkable fact that the Judicial nature of the Alaskan Tribunal is almost completely ignored by the press and politicians of this country" (PRO FO 5/2542, p. 238).

23. PAC Minto Papers (C-3113), vol. I, p. 30, Conversation with Laurier, Feb. 25, 1903.

24. Laurier to Hay, Feb. 24, 1903, Dennett, *op. cit.,* pp. 357-58; Dennett uses the word "futile," answer in PAC Laurier Papers, pp. 71513-16, "Private," March 27, 1903.

25. Hay to Henry White, "Absolutely Confidential," April 10, 1903, Tansill, *op. cit.,* pp. 238-39.

26. Julian Amery, *The Life of Joseph Chamberlain* (London, Macmillan, 1969), vol. 5, p. 139.

27. C. S. Campbell, Jr., *op. cit.,* pp. 314-15. The reference to Lansdowne is in PAC Minto Papers (C-3114) vol. XII, p. 62, Lansdowne to Minto, March 5, 1903.

28. PAC CO 42/892, pp. 163-64, cable paraphrase, "Secret and Personal."

29. Laurier's comment in C. S. Campbell, Jr., *op. cit.*, p. 316; full version of Minto to C.O., March 6, 1903 in PRO FO 414/177, p. 33; edited version in *Can. Sess. Pap.* (No. 46a) 1904, p. 62, and Munro, *op. cit.*, pp. 47-48 and p. 45. My emphasis.

30. PAC CO 42/892, pp. 181-82, minutes of March 7, 1903 and *ibid.*, p. 185, C.O. to F.O., "Immediate," March 7, 1903; Lansdowne's concurrence in PRO FO 414/177, p. 34, F.O. to C.O., "Confidential," March 7, 1903.

31. *Ibid.*, p. 37, "Secret."

32. *Debates,* March 13, 1903; Borden, pp. 33-36; Charlton, pp. 68-75, quotation, p. 73; Bourassa, pp. 86-87; Laurier, pp. 41-44, quotations, pp. 42, 43.

33. PAC CO 42/892, p. 296, March 19, 1903 and *ibid.*, p. 329, minute of Anderson, March 24, 1903.

34. *Ibid.*, pp. 329-31, quotations on p. 329 and in Herbert to Minto, "Personal," March 30, 1903 (PAC Minto Papers, vol. 13, p. 26).

35. PAC CO 42/892, p. 331, March 24, 1903.

36. PRO FO 414/177, pp. 52-53, F.O. to C.O., "Confidential," March 28, 1903; quotations, p. 53.

37. PAC CO 42/894, p. 186, minutes, 30 and 31 March 1903. Chamberlain's failure to comment on the Foreign Office reply and his letter to W. S. Fielding (see below, n. 42) suggests that he did not disapprove of Foreign Office action but that earlier he felt he had to support the Colonial Office in its protest. This also suggests that Chamberlain's absence in South Africa during the making of the Hay-Herbert Treaty was not important. Indeed may not one reason for his absence have been to protect his image vis-à-vis Canada?

38. PRO FO 414/177, p. 56, Chamberlain to Minto, April 2, 1903, cable, inc. in C.O. to F.O., "Confidential," April 3, 1903.

39. PAC CO 42/883, pp. 465-6 to Davis (?); Anderson's emphasis.

40. PRO FO 5/2542, p. 221, presumably 7 March 1903. F. H. Villiers in an undated minute to Lansdowne noted: "You will of course remember how the King insisted upon ratifying. Once his ratification [was] signed we could not delay the exchange. I explained this a few days ago to the Colonial Office." Lord Lansdowne commented: "It was a rather unnecessary proceeding and gives the Canadians an opportunity of which they will avail themselves." See also *ibid.*, p. 235, draft F.O. to C.O., March 10, 1903: "There were special reasons for not delaying formal ratification & this took place on the 17th inst." This was crossed out and in Lansdowne's handwriting the following substituted: "The treaty was accordingly ratified without delay and the announcement made in the speech from the throne. It was not until the [blank] that we heard of the American selections." This change and the comment on the "unnecessary proceeding" suggest that Lord Lansdowne was the author of the Foreign Office manoeuvre.

41. *Op. cit.*, p. 317.

42. March 11, 1903, cited in Julian Amery, *op. cit.*, vol. 5, p. 139 and reply, PAC Minto Papers, vol. 14, pp. 110-11, copy, J. Chamberlain to W. S. Fielding, "Private", April 2, 1903. For another effective answer to Canadian complaints, see also PAC Grey of Howick Papers, vol. 13, pp. 3406-12, memorandum prepared by Sladen (of the Gov.

Gen.'s office) for Grey, Oct. 18, 1905 and inclosed in Grey to Lyttleton, Oct. 18, 1905, "Private." This memorandum was a defence of Britain's position against the attack of Richard Jebb in his book *Studies in Colonial Nationalism* (London, E. Arnold, 1905).

Chapter 6

1. There are American accounts of the tribunal in the principal works cited. C. S. Campbell, Jr., *Anglo-American Understanding, 1898-1903* (Baltimore, Johns Hopkins, 1957), ch. 15 gives a good scholarly account. Primary Canadian accounts may be found in J. W. Dafoe, *Clifford Sifton* (Toronto, Macmillan, 1931), ch. 8 and Maurice Pope, ed., *Public Servant: Memoirs of Sir Joseph Pope* (Toronto, Oxford U. P., 1960), pp. 150-55. See also John A. Munro, *The Alaska Boundary Dispute* (Toronto, Copp Clark, 1970).

2. *Can. Sess. Pap.* (No. 46a), 1904, p. 63, Minto to Chamberlain, March 17, 1903.

3. Dafoe, *op. cit.*, pp. 221-22.

4. To J. W. Foster, April 7, 1903, C. C. Tansill, *Canadian-American Relations 1874-1911* (Toronto, Ryerson, 1943), p. 238, n. 24.

5. Paragraph material based on PRO FO 5/2542 and PRO FO 414/177 Conf. F.O. Print 8296, A.B. Corres., XV in March and April 1903; PAC Laurier Papers, pp. 71257-59; Tansill, *op. cit.*, pp. 239-46; Ms Div., Lib. Cong., Choate Papers, Box 14, Hay to Choate, May 5, 1903 for quotation.

6. PAC Pope Papers, vol. 55, f. 19, May 13, 1903 and PAC Sifton Papers, vol. 273, *passim*.

7. *A.B.T.*, vol. V, part III, p. 29, to Herbert, June 16, 1903.

8. PAC Pope Papers, vol. 55, f. 19, July 28, 1903, report to Sifton; PAC Sifton Papers, vol. 273, June 8, 1903; *A.B.T.*, vol. I, p. 11.

9. *A.B.T.*, vol. V, part III, pp. 28-29, to Herbert, June 16, 1903.

10. *Ibid.*, pp. 27-30; *ibid.*, p. 26, Herbert to Hay, June 12, 1903; *ibid.*, p. 29, Hay to Herbert, June 16, 1903; *ibid.*, vol. IV, part III, p. 5.

11. *Selections from the Correspondence of Theodore Roosevelt and Henry Cabot Lodge, 1884-1918* (New York, Scribner's, 1925), vol. II, pp. 4-5.

12. Howard K. Beale, *Theodore Roosevelt and the Rise of America to World Power* (Baltimore, Johns Hopkins, 1956), p. 130; *Literary Digest*, vol. XXVII (Nov. 28, 1903), p. 727.

13. *Selections, op. cit.*, pp. 32, 35, 37.

14. Tyler Dennett, *John Hay* (New York, Dodd Mead, 1933), pp. 359-60.

15. Beale, *op. cit.*, pp. 124-26; *Selections op. cit.*, p. 39; Allan Nevins, *Henry White* (New York, Harper, 1930), p. 232.

16. Elting E. Morison, ed., *Letters of Theodore Roosevelt* (Camb., Mass., Harvard, 1951), vol. III, pp. 529-31, "Personal," and Munro, *op. cit.*, pp. 56-58.

17. John A. Garraty, "Henry Cabot Lodge and the Alaskan Boundary Tribunal," *New Eng. Quart.*, vol. 24 (Dec. 1951), pp. 471-72 and Beale, *op. cit.*, p. 128; Carman Miller, "Minto and Canadian-American Relations, 1898-1904," typescript, p. 31, paper delivered at Can. Hist. Assoc. meetings, June 1971.

18. Ms Div., Lib. Cong., Hay Papers, Aug. 14, 1903, "Personal & Confidential," for most of the rest of this letter, see Tansill, *op. cit.*, p. 245, n. 61; John A. Garraty, *Henry Cabot Lodge, A Biography* (New York, Knopf, 1943) p. 246.

19. Cited in Hay to Foster, Aug. 5, 1903, Frances M. Phillips, *John Watson Foster* (Doct. Disser., Univ. of New Mexico, 1953) p. 464, n. 79; Tansill, *op. cit.*, p. 245, n. 61.

20. G. W. Monger, *The End of Isolation British Foreign Policy 1900-1907* (London, Nelson, 1963), pp. 125-46, 157-59. The British Conservative Party was also breaking up because of the tariff question.

21. PAC Sifton Papers, vol. 285, "Confidential Opinions of Sir Allen Aylesworth on the Alaska Boundary Dispute" to F. W. Gibson, Oct. 9, 1942, p. 2.

22. Dennett, *op. cit.*, p. 361; Nevins, *op. cit.*, pp. 199-201; "cowboy diplomacy" is from the Louisville *Courier-Journal*, cited in *Literary Digest*, vol. XXVII (Nov. 28, 1903), p. 727.

23. Munro, *op. cit.*, pp. 74-76. Pope's views written Oct. 10, 1903, and postscript Nov. 13, 1903.

24. PAC CO 42/893, pp. 181-84; quotations on pp. 182, 183.

25. Dafoe, *op. cit.*, pp. 228-29.

26. *Selections, op.* cit., p. 69, Oct. 12, 1903; Garraty, "Henry Cabot Lodge . . . ," *op. cit.*, p. 490.

27. Dennett, *op. cit.*, p. 379; *Selections, op. cit.*, p. 61, Sept. 29, 1903, "Confidential."

28. Tansill, *op. cit.*, pp. 258-59, n. 98, "Private and Confidential."

29. Oct. 15, 1903, *ibid.*, p. 257, n. 96 and pp. 257-58.

30. *Selections, op. cit.*, p. 59, Sept. 24, 1903. Lodge also wrote: "We all agreed that if Alverstone decided in our favor on the main contention, namely, the heads of the inlets, that we could afford, *with a slight modification*, to accept their Portland Channel" (*ibid.*), my emphasis; Morison *op. cit.*, vol. III, p. 601; *A.B.T.*, vol. VI, pp. 76-83 *passim*; the decision is in *A.B.T.*, vol. I, pp.

29-32, *Can. Sess. Pap.* (No. 46a), 1904, pp. 65-67, and Munro, *op. cit.* pp. 60-61.

31. Douglas Cole, "Notes and Comments: Allen Aylesworth on the Alaska Boundary Award" (Interviews of J. S. Ewart with Allen Aylesworth, Sept. 9, Oct. 5, 9, 10, 1907) *Can. Hist. Rev.*, vol. LII (Dec. 1971), p. 474; F. W. Gibson, *The Alaskan Boundary Dispute* (M.A. Thesis, Queen's University, 1944), pp. 357-58; but Aylesworth admitted that "Alverstone did what he could with Root and Lodge" (Cole, *op. cit.*, p. 475).

32. Alverstone's argument is in *Can. Sess. Pap.* (No. 46a) 1904, p. 68 and *A.B.T.*, vol. I, p. 34; Gibson, *op. cit.*, p. 362 uses the word "specious" and describes the explanation of the American commissioners on the same subject as "equally flimsy" (*ibid.*, p. 363); and PAC Sifton Papers, vol. 275, T. H. Sanderson to Clifford Sifton, Oct. 27, 1903.

33. Ewart's essay is in John S. Ewart, *Kingdom of Canada . . . and Other Essays* (Toronto, Morang and Co., 1908), pp. 299-347 and excerpts in Munro, *op. cit.*, pp. 66-69; explanation in Cole, *op. cit.*, p. 473.

34. Dafoe, *op. cit.*, p. 233.

35. Lodge to Constance Lodge Gardner, Oct. 11 and ff., 1903, Garraty, "Henry Cabot Lodge . . .", *op. cit.*, p. 494.

Chapter 7

1. PAC Sifton Papers, vol. 285, F. W. Gibson, "Confidential Opinions of Sir Allen Aylesworth on the Alaska Boundary Dispute", Oct. 9, 1942, p. 5 and John A. Munro, *The Alaska Boundary Dispute* (Toronto, Copp Clark, 1970), pp. 62-64.

2. *Alaskan Boundary Tribunal,* vol. I (Ser. No. 4600), p. 87; *Can. Sess.*

Pap. (46a) 1904, pp. 73-93 (p. 75); *Globe*, Oct. 21, 1903.

3. Unless otherwise noted all the newspaper quotations in this section are from J. Castell Hopkins, *Canadian Annual Review 1903* (Toronto, Ann. Rev. Pub. Co., 1904), 365-74 and Munro, *op. cit.*, pp. 88-93.

4. *Debates,* Oct. 23, 1903, pp. 14826, 14828.

5. Cited in Ottawa *Journal,* Oct. 23, 1903; *Debates, op. cit.* p. 14841; Oct. 21, 1903.

6. Nov. 14, 1903 (vol. 61), p. 1926, Ottawa Correspondent, Nov. 2, 1903.

7. PAC CO 42/893, p. 128, inc. in Minto to Lyttleton, "Confidential," Oct. 25, 1903.

8. Victoria Semi-Weekly *Colonist,* Oct. 27, 1903.

9. *Debates,* Oct. 23, 1903: Bourassa, pp. 14773-89; Gourley, p. 14782; Borden, p. 14792; and Munro, *op. cit.,* pp. 100-8.

10. *Debates,* Oct. 23, 1903, pp. 14810-18, quotations, pp. 14814, 14815-16, respecively; PRO FO 414/177, p. 192 (Conf. F.O. Print, 8296, A.B. Corres., XV), Minto's interview with Sir Richard Cartwright, "Secret," Nov. 13, 1903 in Minto to Chamberlain, "Secret," Nov. 18, 1903, inc. in C.O. to F.O., "Secret," Dec. 10, 1903.

11. *Globe,* Nov. 3, 1903 and Munro, *op. cit.,* p. 125.

12. PAC CO 42/893, p. 132, Minto to Lyttleton, cable, Oct. 26, 1903; *ibid.,* p. 130, Oct. 26, 1903; Anderson minute, Oct. 27, 1903 (CO 42/894, pp. 697-98 (B-2218)).

13. PAC Sifton Papers, vol. 275 (C-2173), Alverstone to Aylesworth, Oct. 24 (?) 1903 (H.B.M.G. Conf. Print, Oct. 24, 1903) and cf. id to id, Oct. 21 and 26, 1903; *ibid.,* Aylesworth to Alverstone, Nov. 3, 9, 11, 1903; PAC CO 42/895, pp. 433-39, Alverstone to Laurier, Oct. 30, 1903, inc. in C. O. to F. O., Jan. 22, 1904; CO 42/893, pp. 380-86, Minto to Alverstone, "Confidential," Dec. 8, 1903 and *ibid.,* p. 43370, Minto to Alverstone, Dec. 22, 1903 (latter item cited in Carman Miller, "Minto and Canadian-American Relations, 1898-1904," p. 34, typescript of speech at Can. Hist. Assoc. meetings, 1971).

14. PAC CO 42/893, pp. 387-93 (copy) Laurier to Alverstone, "Confidential," Dec. 22, 1903, inc. in Minto to Lyttleton, Dec. 24, 1903; cf. *ibid.,* pp. 375-378; *ibid.* p. 374 for Anderson comment, Jan. 12, 1904.

15. PRO FO 414/177, p. 186, C.O. to F.O., "Secret," Dec. 10, 1903 and cf. *ibid.,* pp. 184, 195; the Colonial Office apparently made no official reply to Minto's later urging; PAC Minto Papers, Letter Book (A132), pp. 246-47; "Private," Dec. 14, 1903 and *ibid.,* vol. 14, pp. 133-34, "Private," Dec. 28, 1903.

16. PRO FO 414/177, pp. 195-96, Minto to Lyttleton, "Confidential," Dec. 12, 1903, inc. C.O. to F.O., Dec. 24, 1903; PAC CO 537/486 (B-3239), p. 2, to C.O., paraphrase cable, "Immediate, Confidential," Jan. 12, 1904, for Laurier's objections; PAC Minto Papers, Letter Book, vol. 4, p. 282, to Lansdowne, Jan. 12, 1904 and *ibid.,* vol. 12, p. 67, Feb. 4, 1902; for this correspondence see PRO FO 5/2600, FO 414/177, and FO 414/181.

17. A. E. Campbell, *Great Britain and the United States 1895-1903* (London, Longmans, 1960), p. 121.

18. PAC Sifton Papers, vol. 275 (C-2173), Oct. 23, 1903 and *ibid.,* vol. 292, pp. 301-2. Oct. 26, 1903; Ramsay Cook, *The Politics of John W. Dafoe and the Free Press* (Univ. of Tor. Press,

1963), p. 27; vol. XXVII (Oct. 31, 1903), p. 587.

19. Cited in Ottawa *Journal,* Oct. 23, 1903; 37 *ALR* (Nov. 1903), pp. 900-10; the *Review* added: "The shrill shrieking . . . so loud as leads us to believe that the Canadians really thought they were in the right" (p. 910).

20. Cited in *Literary Digest,* vol. XXVII (Oct. 31, 1903), pp. 570-71; reproduced in *Globe,* Oct. 24, 1903, p. 9; Tyler Dennett, *John Hay* (New York, Dodd Mead, 1933), p. 362.

21. PAC Minto Papers, vol. XII, p. 64, "Private", Jan. 11, 1904 and CO 42/894, p. 778, Jan. 4, 1904. Minto reported that feeling (in Government circles) was almost as bitter against Herbert as against Alverstone. Note also, that Choate's speech took place six days after the Panama revolution.

22. Ottawa *Journal,* Nov. 9 and Nov. 11, 1903.

23. Vol. XXVII (Nov. 14, 1903), p. 649; Ottawa *Journal,* Nov. 11, 1903, Toronto *Star* cited in *ibid.,* Nov. 12, 1903; cartoon reproduced in *Lit. Dig.,* XXVII, (Dec. 26, 1903), p. 909.

24. PRO FO 414/177, p. 193, Minto's Conversation with Sir Richard Cartwright, Nov. 13, 1903, inc. in Minto to Chamberlain, "Secret," Nov. 18, 1903, inc. in C. O. to F. O., "Secret," Dec. 10, 1903; PAC CO 42/893, pp. 322-32, Laurier Memorandum, "Secret," in Minto to Lyttleton, "Secret," Dec. 3, 1903. In answer to Minto's skeptical inquiry Laurier reaffirmed his fear that the United States might seize Newfoundland (PAC Minto Papers, vol. 2, p. 61, Conversation with Sir W. Laurier, Dec. 13, 1903); "Pilgrimages to Ottawa, 1903-1913" by A. C. Gluek, Jr., is in Can. Hist. Assoc., *Historical Papers* 1968, pp. 65-83.

25. PRO FO 5/2600 and FO 414/181 Conf. FO Print, A.B. Corres. 1904, XVI, contains the correspondence; quotation in *ibid.,* p. 24, Durand (Sir Mortimer, Br. Amb. to U.S.) to Minto, "Secret," April 14, 1904, inc. in Durand to Lansdowne, "Secret," April 15, 1904; agreements in William Malloy, *Treaties, Conventions . . . 1776-1909* (Ser. No. 5646) (Washington, Govt. Print. Off., 1910), pp. 796-98; for a later American interest in mollifying Canada, see Gaddis Smith, "The Alaska Panhandle at The Paris Peace Conference, 1919" (*Internat. Jour.,* vol. 17 (1961-62), pp. 25-29).

26. New York *Commercial Advertiser,* March 25, 1899, cited in Norman Penlington, *Canada and Imperialism* (Univ. of Tor. Press, 1965), p. 199. F. C. Wade, acting leader of the staff preparing the British arguments, disclosed the adolescent Canadian naiveté in his comment to Edward Blake on July 14, 1903: "We all agree with you here that the U.S. Counter Case is extremely unfair" (Sifton Papers, vol. 274).

27. *Selections from the Correspondence of Theodore Roosevelt and Henry Cabot Lodge 1884-1918* (New York, Scribners, 1925), vol. II, p. 48 and John W. Dafoe, *Clifford Sifton* (Toronto, Macmillan, 1931), pp. 226-27.

28. Speech, May 25, 1911, "Unlimited Arbitration between Great Britain and the United States," Lake Mohonk Conference on International Arbitration, Report No. 17, 1911, p. 124; Neil Compton, "In Defence of Canadian Culture," in Norman Penlington, ed., *On Canada Essays in Honour of Frank H. Underhill,* (Univ. of Tor. Press, 1971), p. 110.

Bibliographical Note

Hitherto the only extensive published and documented account of the whole Alaska boundary dispute appears in the relevant chapters of Charles Callan Tansill, *Canadian-American Relations 1875-1911* (Toronto, Ryerson Press, 1943). The chief value of Tansill's work lies in its voluminous footnotes of manuscript sources — mostly American. John A. Munro's recent paperback *The Alaska Boundary Dispute* (Toronto, Copp Clark, 1970) contains a useful collection of documents and opinions, largely selected from the traditional Canadian point of view. Munro's book forms a valuable contrast to the present work. The basic source, containing both the American and British cases, will be found in *The Alaskan Boundary Tribunal,* Senate Document, No. 162, 58th Congress, 2nd Session, 1903-4 (Ser. Nos. 4600-6) (Washington, 1904), six volumes and five atlases. Though somewhat out of date F. W. Gibson's excellent 450-page master's thesis, *The Alaskan Boundary Question* (Queen's University, 1944), 2 vols., carefully analyzes the printed and considerable manuscript material.

The principal British manuscript sources include the Colonial Office papers, the CO 42 series, copies of which are in the Public Archives of Canada (PAC), and the Foreign Office Papers and the FO Confidential Prints of the Alaska Boundary Correspondence 1886-1907 in the Public Record Office (PRO) London. Charles S. Campbell, Jr., *Anglo-American Understanding 1898-1903* (Baltimore, Johns Hopkins, 1957) lists the numbers of the relevant FO series together with American diplomatic sources, the most important parts of which Tansill, *op. cit.,* quotes in his footnotes. The CO and FO papers, just mentioned, also contain the principal Canadian sources. The other important Canadian sources will be found in the Minto Papers,

Laurier Papers, Sifton Papers, Pope Papers, Klotz Papers, all in PAC.

Biographies containing source material include Samuel Flagg Bemis, *John Quincy Adams and the Foundations of American Foreign Policy* (New York, Knopf, 1949); the biographies of George Canning, Charles Bagot, and Stratford Canning barely touch the boundary question. The biographies and the correspondence of the later American leaders must be consulted: Tyler Dennett, *John Hay, From Poetry to Politics* (New York, Dodd Mead, 1933); Allan Nevins, *Henry White, Thirty Years of American Diplomacy* (New York, Harper, 1930); *Selections from the Correspondence of Theodore Roosevelt and Henry Cabot Lodge 1884-1918* (New York, Scribner's, 1925), vol. 2; Elting E. Morison, ed., *The Letters of Theodore Roosevelt* (Cambridge, Harvard Univ. Press, 1951), vols. 3, 4; John A. Garraty, *Henry Cabot Lodge, A Biography* (New York, Knopf, 1953); P. C. Jessup, *Elihu Root* (New York, 1938). A few British biographies contain a little useful material: J. A. H. Grenville, *Lord Salisbury's Foreign Policy* (London, Athlone Press, 1964); Julian Amery, *The Life of Joseph Chamberlain* (London, Macmillan, 1951, 1969), vols. IV, V; Lord Newton, *Lord Lansdowne* (London, Macmillan, 1929); John Buchan, *Lord Minto* (London, Nelson, 1924). Buchan's book should be used with caution. Adequate biographies of Julian Pauncefote or Joseph Choate do not exist, nor do up-to-date ones of Lansdowne or Hay. Canadian biographies, O. D. Skelton, *Sir Wilfrid Laurier* (Toronto, Gundy, 1921), vol. 2 usefully reflects the traditional Canadian point of view, and John W. Dafoe, *Clifford Sifton* (Toronto, Macmillan, 1931) does so more intensely. Maurice Pope, ed., *Public Servant, Memoirs of Sir Joseph Pope* (Toronto, Oxford, 1960) should also be consulted.

In addition to the foregoing biographies, there are good chapters on aspects of the Alaska boundary problem in John S. Galbraith, *The Hudson's Bay Company as an Imperial Factor 1821-1869* (Berkeley and Los Angeles, Univ. of Calif. Press, 1957); Robert Craig Brown, *Canada's National Policy 1883-1900* (Princeton, Princeton Univ. Press, 1964); Norman Penlington, *Canada and Imperialism 1896-1899* (Toronto, Univ. of Tor. Press, 1965); Howard K. Beale, *Theodore Roosevelt and the Rise of America to World Power* (Baltimore, Johns Hopkins,

1956), pp. 110-31; Charles S. Campbell, Jr., *Anglo-American Understanding 1898-1903* (Baltimore, John Hopkins, 1957); and A. E. Campbell, *Great Britain and the United States 1895-1903* (London, Longman, 1960). The latter two books are especially valuable as background and sources for the last five chapters of this book. The point of view of the former book is American and the latter, British. A useful collection of essays, several directly pertinent to this book, will be found in Morgan B. Sherwood, *Alaska and Its History* (Seattle, Univ. of Wash. Press, 1967).

For a fascinating account of the atmosphere of the later period, see chapters 1, 3, 7 of Barbara W. Tuchman's *The Proud Tower, A Portrait of the World Before the War, 1890-1914* (Bantam Paperback, 1967).

Index

Choate, Ambassador Joseph A.: Alaska, 44, 46; and A.B.T., 84, 85, 88, 89, 91; and "Mt. Herbert," 113; interview and cable, 96-7; sees Laurier, 62-4, 110
Citizen, Ottawa: 107
Cleveland, President Grover: 23, 31, 33, 60-1
Classen, H. George: 123, n. 11
Clayton-Bulwer Treaty: *see* Isthmian Canal
Colombia: 113
Colonial Office: 24, 25, 30, 50, 63; and Minto, 108; supports Canada, 73-4, 76, 77-80, 87; *see also* John Anderson and Joseph Chamberlain
Cook, Captain James: 2
Convention of 1818 (Oregon area): 4, 5, 7, 15
Conservative party and Alaska: 43, 118
Cornwall and York, Duke of: 60
Crimean War: 15

Dafoe, John W.: 84, 111, 117
Dall, Dr. W. H.: 23, 30
Davies, Sir Louis: 49-50
Dawson, Dr. George M.: 23, 30, 31
Dawson City: 34
Denison, Colonel George: 106
Dennis, J. S.: 22
Dingley Tariff, 1897: 33, 42-3
Durand, Sir Mortimer: 66
Dryad incident: 15
Dyea: 34, 38; *see also* Dyea and Skagway
Dyea and Skagway: 41, 43, 44-5, 50, 59

Economist, London: 105
Edward VII, King: 79, 80
Evarts, William M.: 22
Evening Telegram, Toronto: 69-70
Ewart, John S.: 99

Farrer, Edward: 75
Fashoda: 40
Fielding, W. S.: 81
Finlay, Sir Robert (later Lord): 83, 91, 97-8
Fish, Hamilton: 20
Flag incidents: 56-7
Foreign Office: 59, 62, 99; and Hay-Herbert Treaty, 73-80 *passim,* 87, 108, 118, 128, n. 12
France: 2-3, 5-6, 40, 52, 92
Foster, John W.: 39; agent at A.B.T., 85-89, *passim,* 111, 119
Fuller, Chief Justice Melville W.: 70

Gage, Lyman P.: 36

Galbraith, John S.: 15
Germany: 92; and Boer War, 52-3; and Venezuela debts, 67, 68, 71
Gibson, Professor F. W.: 132, n. 32
Globe, Toronto: 107, 113
Gluek, Professor Alvin C.: 67
Goods, transportation of, to Alaska: 36, 56
Gosnell, R. E.: 37, 106
Gourley, S. E., M.P.: 104, 105, 106
Grant, President U. S.: 21
Gray, Justice, J. H.: 8, 21-4, *passim,* 30, 37, 116
Greenland: 112

Hague Court of Arbitration: 68
Harcourt, Sir William V.: 90
Hawaiian Islands: 3, 36, 62
Hay, Secretary of State John: and award, 112-3, 115-6; and Canada, 43-4, *passim,* 47, 55-7, 60, 128, n. 12; and Roosevelt and A.B.T., 88-9, 93, 96-7
Hay-Herbert Treaty: 60, 104, 107, 118; "arbitral" and, 70-1, 130, n. 37; and A.B.T., 88-91
Hay-Pauncefote canal treaties: 53-4, 59, 117; and Clayton-Bulwer Treaty, 40
Hay-Pauncefote draft treaty: 64, 67
Herald, Hamilton: 105
Herald, Montreal: 106, 112
Herbert, Ambassador Sir Michael: and A.B.T., 85, 86; and Minto, 67, 74-5; and Supreme Court, 70-4, 128, n. 11, 129, n. 19, 129, n. 22
Herschell, Lord: 38-39, 41, 105
Holmes, Justice Oliver Wendell: 70, 96
Hudson's Bay Company: 5, 10, 14-15, 17, 49
Hudson Bay: 112
Hunters, Joseph: 22, 116

Indians: 55

Japan: 52, 92; anti-Japanese acts, 43
Jameson Raid: 52, 113
Jebb, Richard: 137, n. 42
Jetté, Sir Louis: 82, 95, 98, 103
Jingoism: 41, 42-3, 46, 48, 89; *see also* anti-Americanism
Joint High Commission, 1887-1888: 25, 30
Joint High Commission, 1898-1899: and Canada, 8, 42, 46, 54, 94, 118; attempted revival, 43-44, 57
Journal, Ottawa: 105
Journal-Post, New York: 113
Juneau: 19, 20

Kannaghunut: 104; *see also* Sitklan and Kannaghunut
Keith, A. B.: 77, 78, 79
King, W. F.: 32, 83, 116
Kitson, Colonel Gerald: 63
Klehini River: 44
Klondike: 10, 34
Klotz, Otto J.: 18, 37, 124, n. 7

Lansdowne, Lord: and A.B.T., 90, 91, 96; and Canada's reaction, 110, 111, 113; and Hay-Herbert Treaty, 66, 71-9, *passim*; as Foreign Secretary, and Alaska, 63-5; as Governor General, 23-4
Latin-American Republics: 5-6
Latitude claims: 4, 6, 7-8, 9
Laurier, Premier Sir Wilfrid: and A.B.T., 82, 83, 88, 95, 100; and Alaska correspondence, 78, 110, 118-9; and award, 105, 107, 108-9, 115; and jingoism, 41, 43, 46; and Joint High Commission, 38, 41; and the United States, 33-4, 115, 117-8
Lewis, Meriwether and William Clark: 2
Lieven, Count: 9, 10
Lincoln, President Abraham: 118
Lindeman, Lake: 38
Lisière: 36, 69; and A.B.T., 88, 94, 97, 99-100, 103; and diplomatic challenge, 17-9, 22-4; demarcation, 116-7
Literary Digest: 69-70, 112, 113-4
Lodge, Senator Henry Cabot: 66; and award, 98-100; and Canada 62, 71, 117; and Roosevelt, 71-2, 88-90, 93-6; photograph, 61
Lynn Canal: 19; and Canada, 34, 37, 39, 40, 46, 95; defeat of claim to, 56, 60, 88
Lyttleton, Alfred: 113

Macdonald, Premier Sir John: 23-4
Mackenzie, Alexander (explorer): 2
Mackenzie, Alexander (premier): 21
Mackenzie and Mann: 37
McKinley, President William: 53, 54, 55, 60, 62
Mail and telegraph tampering: 74
Manitoba School Case: 99
Maps: discussed, 12-14, 49; reproduced, 13, 18, 26-9, 51, 101
Mare clausum: 3
Martin, Peter: 21-22
Mendenhall, Thomas D.: 31, 32
Meridians of Longitude: 8-12, *passim,* 116
Middleton, Henry: 4, 8-9
Miners: 43, 55, 63

Minto, Governor General Lord: and Alaska, 59, 60, 63; and award, 106, 107, 115, 133, n. 15, 134, n. 24; and Hay-Herbert Treaty, 67-9, 73, 74-5, 77; photograph, 58
Modus vivendi: 63; interpretation of, 55; map of, 51; of October 20, 1899, 38, 44, 50, 55, 110, 118
Monroe Doctrine: 6, 8, 53
Montreal: 113
Muir, Alexander: 106
Mulock, Sir William: 63

Napoleon: 3; wars, 2
Nesselrode, Count: 7, 8, 9
Newfoundland: 31, 38, 112, 134, n. 24
New York Times: 112
Nootka Sound: 2

Observatory Inlet: 24
Olney-Pauncefote Treaty, 1897: 57
Ontario lumber law, 1898: 42-3
"Open Door": meaning of, 123, n. 3
Oregon: 5
"Organic Act," 1884 (Alaska): 20
Orthodox Church: 2
Ottawa: 113

Pacific Cable: 43
Panhandle, Alaska: *see* lisière
Paul, Emperor: 2, 7
Pax Britannica: 52
Panama Revolution: 88, 97, 113, 117; cartoon, 114
Pauncefote, Ambassador Sir Julian (later Lord): 44, 53-4, 57, 62, 93
Phelps, Edward J.: 23, 30
Poletica, Pierre de: 7
Police, North-West Mounted: 44, 56
Pope, Joseph (later Sir): 49; and A.B.T. 83, 85, 86-7, 94
Portland: and A.B.T., 94-6, 97-9; Canada, 11, 22-3; Inlet, 56, 57, 103
Port Simpson: 60, 103, 104
Preference: 34
Prisoners, conveyance of: 56
Pyramid Harbor: 39, 41, 45
Porcupine Creek (Chilkat Pass): 44

Racialism: 43, 48, 52, 54
Raikes, A. S.: 110
Republican party: 33; election victories, 39, 53-4, 67; and cf. 64
Reciprocity: 31
Record-Herald, Chicago: 112
Robinson, Christopher: 83
Rocky Mountains: 2, 5
Roosevelt, President Theodore: and award, 112, 113, 117; and Canada, 48-9, 119; photograph, 61; *see also* Hay, Lodge

Root, Elihu: 62, 71, 72, 88, 98
Ross, Fort: 3
Rowlatt, Sidney A. T.: 83, 86
Rush, Richard: 6
Russia: 10, 52, 92
Russian-American Company: 2-3, 15
Russian-American Convention: of 1824, 8-9, 15; of 1867, 17

Sable Island: 122, n. 4
Sackville-West, Sir Lionel: 31, 123, n. 16
St. Elias, Mt.: 2, 8, 39
St. Pierre and Miquelon: 112
Salisbury, Lord: 23, 30-1, 45-6, 57
Sandars, J. S.: 93
Seal rookeries, decline of: 121, n. 4
Seattle: 34
Separatism in Canada, talk of: 107
Sessional Paper (No 46a), 1904, on Alaska: 110
Seward, William E.: 17
Shortt, Adam: 106
Sifton, Clifford: 36; and A.B.T., 82-7, *passim*, 94-5, 99, 100; and A.B.T. award, 103-4, 111, 116, 119; photograph of, 84
Sitka (Novo-Archangelsk): 8, 9, 15, 19
Sitklan and Kannaghunut: physical features, 104; value of, 100, 103-4, 108
Skagway: 34, 64; *see also* Dyea and Skagway
Smalley, George: 62, 63
Smith, Goldwin: 106
Spring-Rice, Cecil (later Sir): 63
Spain: 2, 5; and colonies, 6
Spanish-American War: 36, 53
Star, Montreal: 113-4
Star, Toronto: 113
Stars and Stripes: 113
State Department: 25, 59; *see also* Hay and Roosevelt
Stikine River: 15, 19, 21, 22, 37, 100
Strip: see lisière
Supreme Court and A.B.T.: 70, 74, 78; *see also* Sir Michael Herbert
Surveys: 14; and A.B.T., 97, 99, 115-6; proposed, 21, 22, 23, 30, 31; treaty 1892, 32

Taku River: 99
Tarte, Joseph: 66
Telegraph Creek: 37
Temporary boundary: *see modus vivendi*

Tenable and/or untenable boundary theory: 23, 30, 37, 97, 100
Teslin, Lake: 37
Thornton, Sir Edward: 20
Thompson, Sir John S.: 30, 31, 32
Tittmann, O. H.: 116
Tompkins, Stuart R.: 7, 15-6
Toronto Board of Education, Chairman of: 106
Treadwell Mining Company: 20
Treaty-making power, Canadian demand for: 107
Troops: American, 19, 38, 44; Canadian, 36; Roosevelt and, 62-3, 88, 119
Tupper, Sir Charles: 24, 30, 42, 43, 46
Turner, Senator George: 71, 72, 75, 88; and Sitklan and Kannaghunut, 98

Ukase of 1799: 2, 7
United States: Alaska storehouses, 55-6; and Britain, 33, 53, 54, 71; and Canada, 33, 41, 119-20; Congress, 20, 21, 22, 53, 85; Senate, 37, 54, 59, 71-2; *see also* Hay, Roosevelt, Republican party
Utrecht, Peace of: 121, n. 4

Vancouver: 113
Vancouver, Capt. George: 2, 30, 98, 109
Venezuela: arbitration precedent, 41, 44, 46, 53, 83; debt dispute, 1902, 67, 68, 71; Incident, 1895-96, 25, 33, 84, 88, 117
Victoria: 19, 21
Villiers, F. H.: 91

Wade, F. C.: 83, 134, n. 26
War Department: 19, 36; Acting Secretary of War, 38; Secretary of War, 62, 71-2
Washington, Treaty of (1871): 21, 37, 38
Whalers, American: 112
White, Justice Edward D.: 70
White, Henry: 64, 66, 85, 93, 96
White Pass: 34, 38

Yankee traders in Pacific: 2, 3, 4
Young, Professor McGregor: 113
Yukon: Field Force, 36; Gold Rush, 34-6; railway, 37; trade with, 36, 56, 126, n. 15